TYRTAEUS

Lajos Walder c. 1943

Also by Lajos Walder

Vase of Pompeii: A Play
Below Zero: A Play
The Complete Plays

Lajos Walder

TYRTAEUS

A Tragedy

Translated from the Hungarian
by Agnes Walder

Upper West Side Philosophers, Inc.
New York

Upper West Side Philosophers, Inc. provides a publication venue for original philosophical thinking steeped in lived life, in line with our motto: *philosophical living & lived philosophy.*

Published by Upper West Side Philosophers, Inc. / P. O. Box 250645, New York, NY 10025, USA
www.westside-philosophers.com / www.yogaforthemind.us

Cover Art: Detail from a Greek hydria, ca. 550 B.C.E.

The colophon is a registered trademark
of Upper West Side Philosophers, Inc.

Library of Congress Cataloging-in-Publication Data

Names: Walder, Lajos, 1913-1945, author. | Walder, Agnes, translator.
Title: Tyrtaeus : a tragedy / Lajos Walder ; translated from the Hungarian by Agnes Walder.
Other titles: Türtaiosz. English
Description: New York : Upper West Side Philosophers, Inc., 2017.
Identifiers: LCCN 2016033487 (print) | LCCN 2016045450 (ebook) | ISBN 9781935830368 (pbk. : alk. paper) | ISBN 9781935830399 ()
Subjects: LCSH: Walder, Lajos, 1913-1945--Translations into English. | Tyrtaeus--Drama. | Greece--History--Messenian Wars, 735-460 B.C. --Drama. | GSAFD: Historical drama.
Classification: LCC PH3351.W35 T913 2017 (print) | LCC PH3351.W35 (ebook) | DDC 894/.511232--dc23
LC record available at https://lccn.loc.gov/2016033487

Typesetting & Design: UWSP
Printed in the United States of America

CONTENTS

From your children to your children's children

"That's why poets so often resort to writing plays."
—Joseph Brodsky

TRANSLATOR'S PREFACE

"You must try to work always, under any circumstances."
Dmitri Shostakovich

Lajos Walder (1913-1945), my father—poet, playwright and attorney-at-law, whose Hungarian pseudonym was 'Vándor' ('Wanderer')—was well known as a poet in Budapest in the 1930s; yet he was never known as a playwright. He wrote his plays in the harshest of circumstances and in secret in the early 1940s while intermittently serving in a Jewish forced labor battalion. He wrote them without the slightest chance of having them staged or printed, since by then the works of Jewish artists could, by law, no longer be performed or published in Hungary. Today, we are left with the wistful thought that, in those terrible times, he may have at least lived with the hope that one day his plays might find a home in print and on stage. Indeed, throughout the years of organizing and translating my father's plays, this thought has been my abiding inspiration.

Not only were my father's plays completely unknown in his native Hungary, but even as manuscripts they had no physical presence in that country for twenty-eight years. In 1961, my grandmother Ida Walder brought out my father's unpublished manuscripts to our family, who had emigrated to Sydney, Australia, in 1957. In 1989, I returned to Hungary for the launch of the posthumous publication of a volume of my father's selected poems, entitled *A Poet Lived Here Amongst You*. At that time, I took with me copies of the plays in order to show them to the late Géza Hegedüs, renowned literary critic and professor of drama at the University of Budapest. A year later, in 1990, two of my father's three extant plays, *Tyrtaeus* and *Vase of Pompeii*, were published in their original Hungarian under the title *Pompeji*. His third play, *Below Zero*, was planned for a later publication in Hungary.

In his foreword to *Pompeji*, Géza Hegedüs wrote: "In aesthetic value and nuance, the plays differ from the grotesque tartness

7

of Walder's tragi-comic poems, but they are comparable to them in being the uniquely beautiful creations of an original mind." (My father's complete poems in English were published by Upper West Side Philosophers, Inc. in 2015, under the title *Become a Message: Poems*. That volume also contains a detailed synopsis of my father's brief life, which tragically ended on the day of his liberation from the Gunskirchen concentration camp on May 4, 1945.)

In the early post-war years in Hungary, my mother tried repeatedly to have my father's plays staged. She knew several directors and actors personally—many of them from my father's erstwhile literary circle. One particularly close friend of my father's was a highly gifted actor and director. Season after season, he promised my mother that he would see to it that the plays—starting with *Tyrtaeus*—were performed, but this never eventuated. Finally, when my mother tried to pin him down on a firm date, he said that he would have Tyrtaeus put on, on the condition that he himself be named as the playwright. Following this betrayal, my mother did not try to bring attention to the plays again, especially once communist censorship was in place, which made the eventual success of her endeavors highly unlikely.

We don't know the order in which the plays were written. My beloved mother, died in Sydney in 1973. In my conversations with her about my father's work, the sequence in which the plays had been created somehow never came up. My uncle Imre Walder (the other person closest to my father and his literary legacy) was not present when my father composed the plays. The labor battalion my uncle had been assigned to was sent to the Russian front in early 1942, and by the time he returned to Hungary from Russian captivity, my father was no longer alive. Incidentally, the typewritten original of *Vase of Pompeii* bears a copyright stamp in Hungarian and in French. The date on the stamp is February 10, 1944. Nazi Germany invaded Hungary on 19 March 1944. Plans for the annihilation of the Hungarian Jews were already in place by then.

My father was a certified attorney, who had completed his articles just prior to the official institution of the Jewish laws, which barred Jews from practicing in the professions. Indeed, he made ample use of his knowledge of the law in all three of his plays.

From 1942 onward, we only have a handful of poems from my father. With the future so highly uncertain, and forced labor increasingly robbing him of time, he must have made the decision to give the plays priority. Under the circumstances, he was probably looking for a broader expression of his philosophical beliefs than poetry would have allowed him. He had been familiar with the works of Aldous Huxley, Louis Aragon and Louis-Ferdinand Céline, who had begun as poets and continued in prose; he loved the theater and was influenced by Oscar Wilde and the progressive George Bernard Shaw, as well as by German and French playwrights, such as Victorien Sardou; he was equally aware of the works of the Austrian poet and playwright Hugo von Hofmannsthal and the Belgian dramatist Maurice Maeterlinck. Given the strong emphasis on Greek and Latin education in prewar Hungary, moreover, my father was widely conversant with classical Greek and Roman authors as well as the French classics, especially with the works of Jean Racine. His plays are densely packed with insights so pertinent that they seem universally valid even today.

His "was the most credible voice to express the times between the two world wars," Géza Hegedüs has written about my father's poetry. The same holds true for his plays, and in particular for *Tyrtaeus*. Now—well over seventy years after they were written—*Tyrtaeus*, *Vase of Pompeii*, and *Below Zero* are brand-new plays for the English stage.

In the long battle for recognition of my father's remarkable literary talent, I have often thought of Max Brod. Our stories are not at all parallel. But if Max Brod had heeded the wish of his best friend, Franz Kafka, to have all of his works destroyed after his death, world literature would be that much poorer. Similar thoughts have driven me regarding my father's legacy.

TYRTAEUS

DRAMATIS PERSONAE

TYRTAEUS   a poet who is lame.
THE FIVE SPARTAN EPHORS:
    EUPATOR
    NOSOS
    PHYLO
    TINOS
    PATON
LEUKOS   Spartan youth trainer.
SPARTAN FIGHTERS:
    PHARON
    DYONOS
    MARCONA
    LARGOS
PHOTINA   a woman of Sparta
SPARTAN YOUTH
LUKIANOS   "the whip"
OINOS   standing guard
DEMETRIOS
TEKNON   a blond little boy, looking younger than twelve
THYGENOS
PHYGON
JASON
GYNO   has a flute on him for the line-up
AMINA   an old Spartan midwife
FOUR MESSENEAN PRISONERS
TWO SPARTAN WOMEN
THREE SPARTAN VETERANS
A SPARTAN SPY
A SPARTAN RUNNER
TWO SPARTAN HERALDS
SPARTAN GUARD AT THE OPENING OF THE TENT
SPARTAN SOLDIERS, WOMEN, OLD PEOPLE, CHILDREN,
YOUTHS, TORCHBEARERS AND PALLBEARERS

The scene of the tragedy is Sparta, during the final development of the Messenean wars, approximately 2500 years ago.

ACT I

SCENE 1

A clearing in the woods, on a rocky mountain top. Olive trees in the background. Upstage right is dominated by an enormous boulder. Oinos, one of the boys, is standing guard on top of it. Downstage left a life-size straw dummy stands in front of a fig tree; near the dummy, a few stones on the ground. As the curtain goes up, a spear penetrates the thigh of the straw dummy. It has just been thrown by the boy Thygenos, who is standing opposite the straw dummy. Several other boys stand downstage right with their trainer Leukos in the lead.

LEUKOS: Thygenos, how many times have I told you to aim at his eye. If he gets it there, he's finished, whereas in his thigh it's just a wound instead of blindness or death. Try again.

THYGENOS: I can't do it, Sir. My arm's shaking. I must've thrown it fifty times already.

LEUKOS: Who do you think you are—a babbling Athenian, or some wretched Messenean bastard—that you dare open your mouth to me when your task is to throw the spear. Come forward Lukianos. Give him five good lashes. Did I say five? That's not enough. Let him have three for missing the target, three for being tired and three for babbling. How many is that, Lukianos?

LUKIANOS: (*His face is scratched, guffawing, he comes forward, holding a bundle of sticks in his hand*) I am the whip, Sir. I don't know how to count. I strike until you tell me to stop.

LEUKOS: Bend over, Thygenos. Strike him on the buttocks, Lukianos. (*Lukianos strikes him six times*) Stop! So, Thygenos, you got three for being tired, three for missing the target, and there's three more to come. Do you want me to let them go? (*Thygenos involuntarily quivers, but remains silent*) Answer me, Thygenos! Should I let the rest go? (*Thygenos doesn't speak*) Just say the word and you won't have to endure the last three. (*Thygenos doesn't speak*) Think about it Thygenos—three more, as painful as the other six. (*Thygenos doesn't speak*) Ask me to let them go, then maybe ... just maybe ... (*Thygenos doesn't speak*) So don't talk, just plead with your hands ... (*Thygenos doesn't move*) I can see that you can barely stand the pain. The next three will be like rubbing salt in your wounds. Just say 'no more' ...

THYGENOS: The punishment was nine, Sir. There are three more left.

LEUKOS: A Spartan answer, Thygenos. You might have a tendency to babble, and you might be poor at throwing the spear—but you're clear about discipline. Still, a person who's really disciplined shouldn't babble. A Spartan must give a Spartan answer. Sparse words for sparse words. Too many words are always followed by action. A beating for babbling. You got three for being tired, three for missing the target, and you'll get another three because you yourself said that there were three more left. If you hadn't said a word, I'd have let the last three go. Strike him, Lukianos. (*Lukianos strikes him three times*)

LEUKOS: Enough! Stand up, Thygenos, stand up and laugh. And keep on laughing. Because if you laugh, no one will be able to spread the word that Thygenos cried after just nine blows. Jason, put oil on his back. And at night cover it with herbs.

THYGENOS: (*Straightening up with difficulty*) Sir, I need neither oil nor grass. Hand me the spear. Let me have it. I know I can hit the target now. (*He collapses*)

LEUKOS: Lukianos, take him to the creek and plunge him in the water. He'll come to.

LUKIANOS: (*Awkwardly*) I'd go, Sir, but I have a complaint. Yesterday, as approached Teknon with manly love (*he caresses his scratched face stupidly*) he wouldn't obey.

LEUKOS: Did you hear my command? Go right now. Take him to the creek. When he comes to, you can leave him there. In the meantime, I'll hear it from Teknon. (*Lukianos throws Thygenos onto his shoulder without showing any emotion and goes out stage left*) Teknon, come forward, and tell me the truth about his complaint.

TEKNON: (*Terrified, he comes forward*) Sir, I don't even know what he's accusing me of ... I've only been in the boys' tent for two days ... I was with my mother before ...

LEUKOS: Your self-defense got off to a bad start. A Spartan man can never refer to a woman. If you now bring up your mother as an excuse for your disobedience, one day you could just as easily leave your watch for a harlot. As a youth who has completed his twelfth year you've arrived in the boys' tent, so that in accordance with our ancient custom you could commence your communal upbringing. From now on, it's as if your mother no longer existed for you. Sparta fills her place. And your father is the whip and the bundle of sticks that'll teach you to love and honor your mother: Sparta. Do you understand, Teknon?

TEKNON: Yes, Sir, I do.

LEUKOS: Your hair is far too long, your skin is girlish, and your physique is scrawny. Well, given a few years, you'll realize who your real mother is: the one who gave birth to your scrawniness, or the one who molded you into an athlete. Do you understand that, Teknon?

TEKNON: Yes, Sir. I do.

LEUKOS: You appear to understand a great deal, Teknon. It seems as though your mother not only let your hair grow long, but had often told you that you are clever—cleverer than anyone else's son—since you understand things that you have yet to learn. Do you understand, Teknon?

TEKNON: Yes, Sir. I do.

LEUKOS: Only the son of a slut can be so clever. The son of a slut who's passed onto her child everything she's learned from men. Because only a man can be truly wise. A wench can never gain wisdom. Do you understand that, Teknon?

TEKNON: (*Rebellious with rage*) Yes, Sir, I do understand. But if you say another nasty word about my mother ... (*He pulls out the spear from the leg of the straw dummy and aims it at Leukos*) I'll ... (*Indicating that he'll throw the spear at Leukos*)

LEUKOS: (*Surprised, with a sudden, violent anger, he darts over to him*) What will you do, you scrawny frog? (*He controls himself*) What did you say, Teknon? That you'll throw the spear at me if I continue to foul-mouth your mother? Why, I could twist it out of your hand with no more than a flick. But then all these boys would say: It's easy for him to deal with a child. So I won't do it. But neither will I take back my words. To you, Teknon, your mother is not a slut but a respectable Spartan dame who taught her child to defend her in any circumstance; even if it was contrary to the interests of Sparta. Because, dear boys, I have been placed here by the community of Sparta to raise you, sons who have sprung from the loins of Spartan fathers, to be worthy of them. And who could ever contemplate a son so wicked that rather than taking the example of his fighting father, he sneaks around the broad buttocks of his mother. Evil feelings and intentions hide in one who cannot break away from his mother when his body is already engulfed by the waves of manliness. Such a person, prompted perhaps by animal instinct, hopes to discover womanliness in his mother.

DEMETRIOS: That's disgusting.

LEUKOS: You chose the right word. Short and Spartan. It's disgusting. But if it was only that! Good sons, you know that one day you'll become fighters, because Sparta needs fighters perhaps even more than it needs the gods themselves. That's the reason that we athletes were singled out to communally raise each and every youth of Sparta to become worthy of their fathers. Public confidence has chosen us for this honorable office—the ephors and council of elders; in short, all those who want to ensure that the affairs of Sparta are looked after by us in the best possible manner. Our authority extends to turning all of you with uniform strictness, and irrespective of whose sons you are or what your personal inclinations may be, into loyal fighters for the fatherland. And that is what I'm doing. Because it's not captains we need, but troops who will be obedient in every way and in all circumstances. Blind obedience, therefore, is of the highest merit. Then, an over-excited little monkey comes forward, thinks lovingly of the warm lap of his mother, and when his trainer, in the interest of Sparta, publicly reprimands him—reprimands him, mind you, but doesn't hit him—because it is true, boys, that

I have never personally hit any of you with my superior strength —I just decide on the punishment and choose one of you to enforce it—as I was saying, such a hyped up monkey comes forward and aims a spear right at the heart of his trainer, and in so doing boasts of the greatest sin, which is insubordination. Raise the spear high, Teknon, my boy, let everyone see your shame. I said nasty things about your mother, so let the flame of your revenge hold it high. If your rage had been sincere, you would not have waited for anything, you would have thrown the spear at me that instant. But as things stand, you seem like a lying and weak braggart before these noble, decent, good sons of Sparta. No doubt, you, who place such value on babbling, were glad to hear the flow of my words, hoping that they might turn into something pleasant for you and that I might end up retreating before your sharp spear. Then you, an arrogant adolescent who's just defeated his trainer and regardless of your newcomer status, would instantly become a leader among your peers. Have you grown tired, dear Teknon? Hold the spear higher still. Oh, we have no need of leaders here, only of the kind of soldier who, shoulder to shoulder with another and with many hundreds of others, using identical weapons and identical courage, will charge at the enemy. The fiery ones, those who ignite too fast or burn out too soon, are not needed here. Even among the leaders, the first priority is to be as obedient as the common soldier, who in turn can pledge obedience to them. Hold the spear higher, Teknon, my lad, because this is your opportunity to prove that you're not just a namby-pamby woman's babbling milksop, but a youngster who's so blinded and stubborn that, even to the detriment of Sparta, having stabbed a true and loyal trainer, would obtain satisfaction for his own presumed truth. Just higher still with the spear, dear Teknon, because I want to tell you again that your mother is a whoring bitch—a baser hussy has never existed in all of Sparta, but I am your trainer, who has been entrusted by the community of Sparta, by the noble fathers, the honorable ephors and the wise council of elders, to turn you into the kind of fighter who has neither mother nor father—who has no one, and who, in spite of being sighted, obeys blindly when Sparta's salvation is at stake. Your mother is a whoring bitch, but I am your trainer, Teknon, and if the strength of your spirit is greater than that of your body, then hold the spear higher still and throw it at me. (*He crosses his arms over his chest, and with feet wide apart, turns his back to the boy. Teknon first stares intently at his back, then slowly lowers the spear, which finally drops from his hand. When the spear hits the ground, the boys, who have been frozen throughout, begin to move*)

DEMETRIOS: Look at the braggart. Oh, my commander, you did well to turn your back on such scum of the earth, who is not even worthy of a glimpse from you. I want to be the one to mete out twenty-five lashes to him.

LEUKOS: (*In a slightly languid, victorious and fawning voice*) I'd be disappointed in you, Demetrios, if you'd so easily share the punishment of the worthy with the worthless. Punishment itself is already half the reward, since the trainer metes it out to those whom he considers worthy of improvement. And the endurance of punishment is practically a virtue, since the only ones who take it bravely, are the ones who, having recognized their sin, want to improve themselves. Should I be sharing the punishment of noble Spartan youths with such a worthless fellow? Oh no, Demetrios, his punishment will be that we find him unworthy of it, unworthy of the cane.

PHYGON: (*Darts forward rapturously and stops in front of Leukos*) Sir, whip me!

LEUKOS: Why, Phygon, when you are the kind of example whom every youth can gladly consider his ideal. Did you perhaps make a mistake?

PHYGON: Oh no, my Lord. I merge night with day to discipline myself. But I want you to reward me with a punishment so that I may obtain the virtue of enduring it.

LEUKOS: You're a fine boy, Phygon, but punishment is not the same if we take advantage of it.

PHYGON: (*He grabs hold of the bunch of sticks left there by Lukianos*) Then I'll whip myself. (*Whips himself mercilessly*) Now, my Lord, you will have to punish me because I whipped myself contrary to your wishes.

LEUKOS: You're over-eager, Phygon. And I won't punish you, though it's a fault that can easily make the person, and eagerness itself, seem ridiculous.

DEMETRIOS: Phygon, I admire you so much.

SEVERAL BOYS: We can never be worthy of you.

LEUKOS: Get back into line, Teknon. Demetrios will teach you the exercises.

DEMETRIOS: You put him in good hands, my Lord. He'll get more beating than food.

LEUKOS: Be fair, not forceful. This boy might not be such bad material after all. With him, you'll get further with brains than with force.

DEMETRIOS: I don't understand you, my Lord, but I'll do as if I did. And instead of his bum, I'll beat discipline into his head.

LEUKOS: (*Laughing*) You are a cunning fellow, Demetrios. It's no accident that I made you the leader of the group. Cunning is a leader's virtue. With the right words, you'll even get him to do what Lukianos couldn't get from him by force. At least now I know why his face was so badly scratched this morning. (*They laugh*) So, let's see what you stole for the soup today.

DEMETRIOS: A skinny piglet, but we almost came to grief.

LEUKOS: Take care, Demetrios, that they don't catch you. The punishment can be extremely severe. A youth like you cannot endure fifty lashes. It would kill you.

DEMETRIOS: It's a curious thing, Sir, that stealing is allowed, but if the thief gets caught, he might as well commend himself to the mercy of the gods. Why is that?

LEUKOS: Stealing is a pleasant pastime, isn't it, Demetrios? To take from another what he has worked hard for, feels good. But since the punishment of a thief, if caught, is severe, this pleasant pastime is also extremely dangerous. Elsewhere, thieves are the most cowardly, but with us, only the bravest steal, because one must have enormous courage to stake one's life on a few apples or some bad poultry. We Spartans revolve in constant danger;

therefore, we have to live dangerously, so we can train ourselves for the dangers that lurk all around us. You can hardly fulfill the imperative to live dangerously more thoroughly than by risking your life to obtain everything that goes into your daily soup. This state makes you so alert that in a split-second you're ready to overthrow anyone who threatens your life. Stealing is allowed, and it is not shameful, but the clumsy thief goes under. He could pay with his life for a chook.

DEMETRIOS: I still have goose bumps on my back, that's how close I was to being caught yesterday.

OINOS: (*Thus far he's been silently standing guard on the boulder— enthusiastically now, as one who finally has something to report*) My Lord, my Lord, our fighters are bringing captives this way. They have just passed the running tracks. They are coming this way.

LEUKOS: Captives! At last we've got some captives again. It looks as though the affairs of Sparta are turning for the better.

JASON: Their number could be a thousand, Oinos.

OINOS: A thousand, how many is that, my Lord ... because I only see five?

LEUKOS: There'll be more, Oinos. Wait, I'm coming up. (*He starts to climb up the cliff*)

PHYGON: (*Picks up a nearby stone and turns in the direction of Leukos with deadly excitement*) My Lord, I'll crush their heads with this very stone. I'll gouge their eyes out with my nails. Because their cheeks are like the jowls of horses, and they have the hearts of wolves. They devour babies.

JASON: (*With profound respect*) How do you know that, Phygon?

PHYGON: That's what they say. Oh, beloved Sparta! Awful Huns have ambushed our beautiful fatherland.

DEMETRIOS: Calm down, Phygon, Sparta will be triumphant.

OINOS: (*Downwards to the approaching Leukos*) I know how to count to ten ... but they're only five ... and their cheeks are not like the jowls of horses.

PHYGON: (*Screaming*) But they are, if I say so, and they number a thousand!

JASON: Perhaps you know, how many is—a thousand?

PHYGON: (*Screaming*) Their number is a thousand. You stupid doubters. Sparta never takes less than a thousand prisoners.

JASON: (*Conciliatorily*) If Phygon says so, it's good enough for us.

LEUKOS: (*On top of the cliff, he looks around*) Perhaps the light has dazzled my eyes. I can't see them.

OINOS: There ... over there ... my Lord. That large cliff where we practice jumping is hiding them just now. Their number is only five, and their cheeks are not like the jowls of horses.

PHYGON: (*Screaming*) Their number is a thousand, and they have the hearts of wolves. They devour babies. My Lord, with this very stone ...

LEUKOS: (*Bored with it*) You'll crush even a thousand, I know. Aha! I can see them now. For sure, there are only five coming this way. But their number could even be a thousand. Spread the news that we have captured thousands and thousands of prisoners. It will give new strength to the population ...

PHYGON: I'll spread the news everywhere. Thousands and thousands of new prisoners have arrived in Sparta. (*Goes out upstage stage right, behind the cliff*)

OINOS: (*Yells after him*) Don't you even want to see them? They are only five, and they look like men, not horses.

LEUKOS: Quiet, Oinos! (*To the boys*) You do know how prisoners are dealt with? They are to be tortured and tormented.

OINOS: These ones can barely stand on their feet, and they don't look like horses.

LEUKOS: One more word out of you, Oinos, and you'll get ten lashes. (*He continues talking to the boys*) Whoever gives them water or food brings the death penalty upon himself. We do not fatten the enemy who threatens our lives. And no one is allowed to talk to them or fraternize with them, because only cowards get taken prisoners. The courageous ones fight to the death. Talking with these cowards is a sin twice over. In former times, we never took prisoners. We did not chase after the fleeing enemy. But these days we must replenish the slaves because so many of the rascals have escaped. These ones would also escape if they could. So treat them mercilessly. Here they come, move back all of you, lest they should breathe on you. (*Runs down from the cliff and pushes his way through the boys who are backing to the right. He stands at the head of them and raises his arm in a Nazi salute. From upstage left, Pharon and Dyonos arrive with the five prisoners of war, including Tyrtaeus*) Greetings, Pharon and Dyonos, noble fighters! Greetings to you and victory to Sparta!

DYONOS: (*To the prisoners, some of whom have terrible wounds*) Men! ... Whoa, we're stopping here. (*The prisoners collapse on the ground with the exception of Tyrtaeus who is waiting for something ...*)

TEKNON: Terrible ... what shocking wounds.

JASON: I can't understand ... he calls them men.

OINOS: And they look like men, not horses.

DEMETRIOS: (*He doesn't believe his eyes*) One ... two ... three ... four ... five.

LEUKOS: Greetings to you, noble fighters.

DYONOS: (*To the boys, who are creeping forward*) Back off kids. (*To the prisoners*) We'll rest here. You can have half an hour. (*This time, with a slow sigh, Tyrtaeus also lowers himself*)

LEUKOS: (*A little indignant*) Greetings to you, noble fighters.

PHARON: Never mind that. Just give us something to eat instead.

LEUKOS: Your talk is out of line. Victory to Sparta.

PHARON: Idle phrases. Instead of feeding our bellies. Greetings and victory! We've heard it all before.

LEUKOS: (*Shocked*) I don't believe it. Could this be Spartan discipline?

PHARON: (*With an outburst*) We rotted in mud. Okay. There were no rags to cover our wounds. Okay. We filled our bellies with grass. Okay. Instead of attacking, we are retreating. Okay. Sooner or later we'll die like animals. Okay. And now this one, here behind the frontlines, demands discipline from us ...

DYONOS: Very well. At least bring water. For them as well ...

LEUKOS: (*Infuriated*) Think of our articles of war. Whosoever gives water to the prisoners betrays Sparta.

PHARON: What are you preaching about. Our orders are to get

them to headquarters alive, parade them through Sparta so that the population can be inspired at the sight of them.

TEKNON: I wish they had jowls like horses, then I could detest them. As it is, I can only feel sorrow. I could cry.

DYONOS: Because you're a decent kid.

LEUKOS: (*Hissing*) Put some sense into him, Demetrios. (*Demetrios punches his fist into Teknon's face. Tyrtaeus shivers involuntarily*)

PHARON: That's how it's meant to be. Whosoever is decent must be punched decently in the head.

LEUKOS: (*Alluding to the boys*) At least show them a good example.

PHARON: (*Furious*) You do it. I've been fighting for three years without a break. Change places with me. And I'll teach the kids to know that when a fighter asks for water, they should bring it immediately.

DYONOS: (*Pulls the ear of Demetrios, who stands next to him*) Hey kid, bring water. Did you hear me? We have our orders, and without water we won't get very far.

1st PRISONER: (*Pointing to Teknon*) You, blond little one. Be merciful and strike me through the heart.

LEUKOS: (*Grasping the psychological effect*) All of you, spit on them. Do you hear me, Jason.

JASON: My Lord, I can't spit. My mouth is dry.

2nd PRISONER: Water!

LEUKOS: Gyno, let's hear the line-up. (*Gyno blows a signal on his flute, and the boys slowly stand in line*)

DYONOS: What about the water?

LEUKOS: You can get it yourselves—traitors!

DYONOS: (*Suddenly furious*) You're telling me that ... You ... I ... (He wants to attack him, but is restrained by Pharon)

PHARON: (*After Dyonos has come to his senses*) You want to start with them? Those homebound sages, who know everything better ... That an attack from the wing should've been done in such and such a way, and the frontal attack just so. How we should've taken advantage of a certain path or occupied a particular height, and, mainly, how to win, win, always win! Because they know just how to do it. And why wouldn't they know, when they have excellent connections everywhere. And that is the truth. How else could they have managed to stay at home ...

LEUKOS: My work is more important ...

PHARON: You pathetic coward, you've just uttered the loafer's slogan. Yeah, you would gladly go, wouldn't you, if your work here wasn't even more important than fighting? But you cannot go, by the gods, you can't, because no less than the salvation of the fatherland rests in your hands. (*To the boys*) Right turn, forward march. Go and hide your master well. Though I swear upon the gods that pretty soon even you will be needed out there, because it is no longer about victory but about survival.

LEUKOS: (*To the boys*) Go to the cliff. I'll be making my report.

PHARON: Why don't you do that? Do that! Just one more thing: In the meantime, I'll stuff my face, and then perhaps discipline will come back to me. And then, who'll believe you that a Spartan soldier, who serves at the front, could speak in a way other than what's prescribed. Hey, Chief, isn't it true that even you couldn't believe it? As you said, it's inconceivable from the mouth of a Spartan soldier! (*In the meantime, following a sign from Leukos, the boys reluctantly start marching off*) It would be a disgrace of such proportions that to speak of it would be a worse sin than to have committed it.

DYONOS: (*Grinning*) You do have a tongue!

PHARON: (*After they're gone*) Believe it or not, I hate his kind more than I hate the enemy. Because I know about his kind, who they are, what they are doing and why. Whereas with the enemy, I only know what they're doing—not who they are and why they're doing it. Believe me, when I think that his kind will also drop dead, I'm sometimes glad that we are losing this war.

2nd PRISONER: Give us water. Water. We too believe in the same gods.

PHARON: You hear that, Dyonos? At least the enemy refers to our common gods, whereas such a loafing rascal would even disavow his own kind in the name of discipline—which means nothing other than blindly serving his own safety.

TYRTAEUS: Bring water, otherwise my companions will perish.

DYONOS: Shut up, lame one. How dare you ask for water from a Spartan? You think I haven't heard you cursing Sparta all the way? You didn't even keep it to a whisper. That we are merciless and evil.

TYRTAEUS: I'm not asking for myself, but for my companions.

PHARON: Don't be such a busybody. Aren't you thirsty? Maybe you're not even tired, that's how come you're always speaking on behalf of your mates. Lame as you are, you did better than all of them on two good legs. You didn't walk like a captive. You walked as though you were going home. You're very suspicious lame one, very suspicious.

TYRTAEUS: Your suspicion is justified. I hate Sparta and that hatred compels me not to accept any favorable treatment from you. Bring water for my companions. Because they won't reach the goal without water. I (*in a prophetic voice*) will get there, even without water.

DYONOS: (*A touch terrified*) Just you wait, I'll get the water, but you won't get a sip of it. Why couldn't such a brazen one be stabbed to death on the way?!

PHARON: Let it be, Dyonos. We finally managed to round up five wounded men, whom we've ceremoniously proclaimed to be prisoners of war. Now, all of Sparta awaits them for great victory celebrations. All five of them have to get there. They are so precious that if one of them dies, we'll have to carry him.

TYRTAEUS: Did you hear that, Dyonos. It's quite straightforward.

DYONOS: Damn this rotten world in which a Spartan has gotten to the stage of needing to worry about the physical wellbeing of the enemy.

TYRTAEUS: Such talk cools my palate. But the others need water. Bring them some.

PHARON: There's bound to be a creek nearby. Go towards the olive trees. Here, you can put some into my helmet as well. (*He hands Dyonos his own helmet*)

DYONOS: (*Grumbles*) All right. All right. Though you could also be going. (*He goes out upstage, between the olive trees*)

TYRTAEUS: Your helmet still sparkles, your shield is immaculate, your spear is without a spot of rust and you grease your sandal straps daily, in accordance with regulations. But where has your toughness gone, that toughness which is known throughout the world as Spartan.

PHARON: Am I not tough, lame one? Here, feel these muscles.

TYRTAEUS: Your arms, your heart and your lungs are still the same. That's why you can still endure the suffering. But the stuff that made you tough inside is missing.

PHARON: Nothing's missing. You're lying! My belief in a Spartan victory is unshakeable. If I could just fill my stomach again, I swear I'll cut down a hundred of your kind.

TYRTAEUS: And if you can't fill your stomach?

PHARON: Then I don't know what will happen. (*He points to his stomach*) Because this emptiness must be filled, otherwise my spine will snap in two.

TYRTAEUS: Apart from filling your belly, doesn't your life mean anything to you?

PHARON: What do you mean?

TYRTAEUS: Do you have a family?

PHARON: I don't have anyone.

TYRTAEUS: If you don't even have food, then what ties you to Sparta? Why are you fighting for it, why are you starving?

PHARON: Because I'm a Spartan.

TYRTAEUS: And what does being a Spartan mean to you?

PHARON: Well ... that ...

TYRTAEUS: You don't know, do you? Then why are you doing this? Why don't you desert them? There's plenty of food on the other side. Abandon the flag!

PHARON: What flag?

TYRTAEUS: The Spartan flag.

PHARON: That I will not do. I'd rather keel over from hunger.

TYRTAEUS: I get it. Though you have no one; though you don't know what ties you to Sparta, or why you're fighting and starving; though you can't feel what it means to be a Spartan—you'd still rather keel over from hunger than abandon it. Don't you see how hopeless this is, or how barren and aimless your life is? It doesn't even mean enough for you to escape starving to death.

PHARON: It's so hard to understand. Can it all be: 'no', 'haven't' and 'nothing'? No, that cannot be. If you had seen how beautiful it was when a thousand divisions goose-stepped at the parade, in front of the leader. A thousand times fifteen men. The crests of their helmets were shining. Their bellies were full; shoulder was taut against shoulder. And the earth thundered. Yes, now I do know what being a Spartan means to me.

TYRTAEUS: (*Realistically*) And what remains of the thousand divisions?

PHARON: Not even a hundred perhaps.

TYRTAEUS: And your belly?

PHARON: Empty.

TYRTAEUS: But your helmet still gleams. That's all that's left of it. Believe me, everything you told me is just appearance! And how much you are all to be pitied that you'd sacrifice your lives for such a dazzle. Strictly speaking, you are not even human beings, because you bear the burden of your awful obsession as if it were natural. Who is the demon who forced upon you the kind of command against which you can't rebel, because it seeped into your blood and is spreading like poison throughout your body. How can I explain this to you? How can I depict the lie—when you don't even know the truth you believe in. One can fight against something, but how does one apprehend nothing? What can I do to wake you up? Should I speak of freedom, or justice, or truth, when it doesn't mean more to you than to prompt you to ask: what for? Oh, if only there were scientists among you, or poets or sculptors ...

PHARON: What for?

TYRTAEUS: To teach you about all the things that represent the meaning of life. I told you before that I hate you. But only now do I realize how much you are to be pitied. A people who live in ignorance under the command of a lying tyrant—a people who have sunk into delusion—an uneducated lot who haven't yet found a teacher.

PHARON: If I didn't know that you're the enemy, I'd have to think that you were born a Spartan. You talk of betrayal with such fervor that it smacks of betrayal against yourself. You want me to betray Sparta so that I can improve my lot? With you, one really can't tell whether your outstretched arm will hit you on the head or support you under the arm. (*Jumps up*) What's that? Did you hear that noise?

3rd PRISONER: Water. Water.

PHARON: Pssst! Quiet. (*Jumps across the stage and grabs someone from behind the cliff*) By the gods, anyone as stealthy as this can only have base intentions! (*He drags Teknon out*) It's you! And why did you come back?

TEKNON: (*Carrying a basket in one hand*) Please, my Lord, no noise. If they catch me, they'll whip me. Though I don't even mind if they whipped me to death for this. I stole some cheese and bread for you from the boys' tent.

PHARON: (*Roughly*) Did you bring it for me or for them?

TEKNON: (*Simply*) I brought it for all who are called men.

PHARON: Just what do you mean?

TEKNON: My Lord, you and your comrade are men. (*Alluding to Dyonos*) Didn't your comrade call out before: "Men! Whoa ... men ... we're stopping here."

PHARON: Now I get it.

TEKNON: I just want to ask you to eat quickly because there are many on their way here.

PHARON: You rustled this up, you be the one to share it around.

TEKNON: The first portions of the cheese belong to you and your comrade. (*He's cutting up the cheese*) I'll break the bread into seven pieces. (*He is breaking up the bread*) You go on and eat and I'll be on watch. Okay?

TYRTAEUS: Would you tell your name to a slave?

TEKNON: My name is Teknon. My mother taught me that slaves are also human beings.

TYRTAEUS: Does such a mother still exist in Sparta. Then all is not lost. (*Dyonos arrives upon the last sentence. He is carrying two helmets filled with water*)

DYONOS: We'll drink to that. Though I've already drunk myself to bits. Did you leave me something from the feast? Look at that. The lame one is also eating the bread of Sparta. There, have some water. Go on. Drink. If you can give away your beliefs for a piece of cheese.

TYRTAEUS: I accept nothing from the enemy. But I'll eat the bread of one who says that slaves are also human beings.

SCENE 2

The tent of ephor Eupator. Large empty walls made of cloth. Downstage right is a bed made of straw. Center stage there are a few logs of wood leaning together. Stage left side near the entrance is a cresset. Upstage center on the wall of the tent hangs something like a map. Eupator is standing alone when Phygon bursts in.

PHYGON: They are bringing prisoners to Sparta. There are thousands and thousands of them. They have the jowls of horses and the hearts of wolves.

EUPATOR: Calm down, young Spartan and tell me the circumstances.

PHYGON: Isn't it enough, my Lord? That so many were captured? Leukos told me to spread the news. (*He is about to rush off*)

EUPATOR: Stay where you are! Who saw them?

PHYGON: I did, my Lord.

EUPATOR: Only you ...?

PHYGON: Others as well. But none with the same feelings ...

EUPATOR: Are you different from the others?

PHYGON: I'm the same as the others on the outside, but inside ...

EUPATOR: What are you like inside?

PHYGON: A thousand prisoners arrived in Sparta. This is the news I have to spread. Ephor, let me continue on my way ...

EUPATOR: Just tell me what you're like inside?

PHYGON: Inside ... inside ... I'm different, but I can't explain it.

EUPATOR: Are you better or worse than the others?

PHYGON: I don't know. But I feel that I am unworthy of being called a Spartan.

EUPATOR: You don't appear to be unworthy of it!

PHYGON: I don't, do I? Yet that is how I feel. Because being a Spartan must be an awfully good feeling. And that's not how I feel. That's why I torment myself.

EUPATOR: What is your name? Whose son are you?

PHYGON: My name is Phygon. I am the son of a dead man and the grandson of a living one.

EUPATOR: Where did your father die?

PHYGON: Where a Spartan usually dies. In battle.

EUPATOR: Your grandfather?

PHYGON: He lives for Sparta. He lives to fight.

EUPATOR: The other way around perhaps. He fights in order to live.

PHYGON: Not so, ephor. He lives to fight. He is the commander.

EUPATOR: (*Surprised*) Are you the grandson of Nosos?

PHYGON: Yes, my Lord.

EUPATOR: Are you the one who hit your mother because she didn't get up to work after giving birth to your little brother.

PHYGON: Yes, my Lord.

EUPATOR: You're the one who eats dirt from the ground?

PHYGON: Yes, my Lord. Because I love Sparta above all.

EUPATOR: Who taught you to do this? (*Nosos enters the tent*)

NOSOS: I did.

PHYGON: (*Yells out*) Thousands and thousands of prisoners arrived in Sparta.

NOSOS: Phygon, my boy, only five.

EUPATOR: (*Disappointed*) Only five ...?

PHYGON: I shall stuff up my ears, so I won't hear this. (*He puts *his hands to his ears and crawls on his knees in front of them*) Kick me. Grind me into the ground, but their number is even more than a thousand. I see as many as there should be, because I love Sparta more than you do. (*In a fit of hysterics, he keeps on smashing himself against the ground*)

EUPATOR: This kid is mad!

NOSOS: He's not mad. He just loves Sparta to the point of madness. (*Gently*) Get up, my boy ... (*Phygon continues to roll and grovel on the floor. Nosos kicks him cruelly. Phygon cries out in pain. He attempts to straighten up, but can't. He crawls out on all fours*)

EUPATOR: (*Astonished*) I don't understand you, commander Nosos. You spoke to him so gently and then you kicked him without mercy.

NOSOS: Because an order from the commander must be obeyed immediately.

EUPATOR: (*After some silence*) Have you brought us good news from the battlefield?

NOSOS: News from the battlefield is not as agreeable as the progress we've been making in enforcing discipline. In the last eight days, only twenty-two men had to be whipped to death for not keeping their weapons clean.

EUPATOR: (*With an outburst*) Commander, you are crueler to your own troops than to the enemy. You're retreating from the enemy while you're annihilating your own.

NOSOS: Discipline comes first.

EUPATOR: Victory comes first.

NOSOS: For the sake of victory, we must first triumph over ourselves.

EUPATOR: If you continue to triumph over us much longer, there won't be anyone left to be victorious against Messene. The severity of your disciplinary actions makes for a greater gap in our lines than the bloodiest assault of the enemy.

NOSOS: In the first place, I am cleansing our army of those whose morals have been undermined by the long war. It's better to lose the war than to allow any relaxation of discipline.

EUPATOR: Commander Nosos, you can't be serious.

NOSOS: I am so serious that if it were up to me, you too would not avoid your fate.

EUPATOR: Nosos, don't lose sight of the fact that you are a commander only in battle. The war is conducted by the people of Sparta. And we, the ephors, are their leaders.

NOSOS: I know, I know. That's why to this day I have to struggle with discipline because I'm being sent such people from the rear.

EUPATOR: (*Conciliatorily*) We know how difficult your situation is due to the overwhelming strength of the enemy.

NOSOS: You make my situation difficult, because you conduct the affairs of Sparta in a manner that would shame our ancestors. The last offense was when you decided not to re-enlist the wounded. A one armed soldier is still capable of fighting.

EUPATOR: It was the wish of the people. They are disgruntled.

NOSOS: The ones who are disgruntled must perish. That's why I said that discipline comes first. Because without it we cannot win. And if we win without it, the very reason we're fighting for—the ancient spirit of Sparta, would perish. The surest guarantee of victory is discipline. It must be loved because if it falls apart we will also fall apart. But if it's only the war we lose, discipline can still do miracles, and Sparta can rise again.

EUPATOR: I too subscribe to this, Nosos, but ...

NOSOS: There is no but. With fire and brimstone if need be, I'll bring about the ancient discipline of Sparta! Not the discipline of yesterday or the day before yesterday, but that of hundreds of years ago.

EUPATOR: I myself have no wish to depart from the spirit of the ancients. But look around you. Look how much progress the world has made since then. In Athens for example ...

NOSOS: There isn't an example that would interest me. And let us not make any progress if it means the slightest alteration to the ancient laws of Lycurgus.

EUPATOR: Oh, no one would dare do that. But the laws can be interpreted in such a way that they'd be more suitable to modern times ...

NOSOS: The laws are clear. There's no need for interpretation.

And progress must be halted if that's what it takes to maintain our world.

EUPATOR: But that's just why they're taking up arms against us. That's why they want to vanquish us. Because they think that we're in the way of progress. In the first place, therefore, we must win.

NOSOS: We will win, once we've reinstated discipline. My time is short. I came to tell you to call up the veterans between the ages of fifty-five and sixty. And you must lower the age limit to twelve.

EUPATOR: Is this necessary for victory?

NOSOS: It's far more necessary than your questions.

EUPATOR: What should we do with the prisoners, commander?

NOSOS: Execute them by morning.

OINOS: (*Runs in out of breath*) Great Lord, they are bringing Demetrios.

EUPATOR: Bringing him? Why doesn't he come himself?

OINOS: We were jumping off the cliff, and he took a bad step and fell off. He might already be dead.

EUPATOR: Dead, Demetrios ... my son ... (*He staggers for a moment, then realizes that Nosos is watching him*) If he is dead, we'll bury him in the appropriate manner. I'll have the prisoners executed by morning, commander.

NOSOS: Hail and victory!

EUPATOR: Hail and victory!

SCENE 3

Still in the tent of Eupator; it is the middle of the night. Stage left, at the entrance to the tent, a flame blazes in the cresset. Eupator and Tyrtaeus stand at some distance from each other.

EUPATOR: Come closer, lame one, let me have a good look at you. (*Tyrtaeus takes a hobbling step*) They tell me that when my son broke his leg, you bandaged it to a piece of wood. Why did you do it? Given that you're an enemy of Sparta?

TYRTAEUS: I'm not an enemy of those who suffer.

EUPATOR: Did you also bandage a wounded enemy on the battlefield? Or were you only merciful with the son of ephor Eupator? Answer me!

TYRTAEUS: Ephor, a name more hated than yours hardly exists in the world. How could anyone hope for your mercy when you are merciless. When things go badly, one doesn't gamble with luck. If your son were to die now, everyone would say that I put poisonous grass on his wounds. My fate would be sealed. Had my aim been merely to win your favor, fear of failure would've squashed my eagerness. But when they brought your son in agony, all else disappeared around me and I saw only a wounded person. I listened solely to my heart, and not to the warnings of the cautious brain. Anyhow, great Lord, how much could your pardon amount to for a Messenean slave. Instead of both ears, you'll only have one chopped off. But there isn't a pardon on earth that could plug up the other ear so well that I would not hear the sound of Sparta's cruel whip upon the suffering. Nor one that could prevent the death rattle of slaves from waking me out of the deepest sleep.

EUPATOR: The things you've said about Sparta and myself are like a hailstorm that shatters the basic crop of Spartan existence, so that nothing but a field of hatred remains in its place. That's how all of you think of Sparta. But let's change the subject. Tell me who taught you the knowledge of wounds. Are you a healer?

TYRTAEUS: I am not a healer in the sense that you think, great Lord. I am the soul's healer. A philosopher. I would like to make life endurable for people—therefore I'm a poet. And because I want to show a better path upon which to travel —I am a teacher. I am not a healer of the body. I just have a grasp of dealing with wounds, in the same way that I have a grasp of proper taxation or of the digging of ditches. If one wants to show the way, great Lord, one has to have some knowledge of even the most menial work. If one wants to build shelter for humanity, one has to know how much pay the clay mixing laborer needs to provide for his family in a dignified manner.

EUPATOR: Slave, the manner in which you speak is unusual for us. So is the patience with which I listen to you. Do not abuse it. Stick to the subject.

TYRTAEUS: I do have a need of my nose, great Lord, so from here on, I'll only reply to your questions.

EUPATOR: (*Without noticing the allusion*) Just tell me how my son broke his leg.

TYRTAEUS: I don't know, ephor. On our way from the battle-field, we rested on a clearing between the cliffs, where the boys were doing their drills. When we arrived, their trainer led them away so we wouldn't contaminate them. I heard that they went to do their exercises on a large boulder. Then suddenly, in the midst of much wailing they brought your son, pale as death, and with a broken and bleeding leg. They were so terrified that they allowed even the enemy to bandage him.

EUPATOR: There, see, you can speak naturally —simply. The Spartan way.

TYRTAEUS: That's true, great Lord. Spartan speech is simple— little short of being excessively so. A Spartan father has never yet left a greater inheritance to his son than three hundred words. But hitting, kicking and stabbing you all know how to do in thousands of variations.

EUPATOR: Again, you spoke without being asked. What manner of person are you?

TYRTAEUS: I am a citizen of Messene, my Lord.

EUPATOR: Did you always live in Messene?

TYRTAEUS: Yes, I am a Messenean.

EUPATOR: You said that already! But was your country of birth somewhere else?

TYRTAEUS: (*A touch taken aback*) No my Lord ... in Messene! But allow me to follow your question with my own. Why did you ask me about my country of birth when I told you that I am a Messenean?

EUPATOR: (*Bitterly*) Because these days many of those who fight under the Messenean flag rally under it only to fight against Sparta, since the way Messene heralds this fight against us is as if it were to the common benefit of all the tribes to vanquish us.

TYRTAEUS: This is a battle of democracy, my Lord ...

EUPATOR: How's that? Would you be the ones who call yourselves democrats? You, among whom one bends over double in front of another? Equality exists only in Sparta. Do you understand that, slave? (*Enraged he smashes into his face*)

TYRTAEUS: I do, my Lord. Your arguments are so convincing. (*He caresses his nose*) And now I find it quite in order that you cut off the noses of disobedient slaves. At least then it can't hurt their noses when you smash them there if they argue with you.

EUPATOR: I must say that was below my dignity, slave. I am not in the habit of living with the methods of the secret police. I was overcome by bitterness. Why is it that all the other countries have left us to ourselves; that no one ever volunteers to fight for our beliefs.

TYRTAEUS: Of true volition, one can only fight for a just cause.

EUPATOR: Are you saying that ours is not a just cause? Take care slave, don't enrage me!

TYRTAEUS: My Lord, do you want to box or to philosophize?..

EUPATOR: Let's do it your way. But I feel that the world isn't fair to Sparta.

TYRTAEUS: Why do you think that?

EUPATOR: Well, because no one's helping!

TYRTAEUS: Help Sparta? But you would never accept it.

EUPATOR: Of course not.

TYRTAEUS: I get it. By now even that would make you feel good—just to be able to refuse the help offered ...

EUPATOR: That's it ...

TYRTAEUS: Or perhaps you're at the point where you wouldn't even refuse it any more.

EUPATOR: You're becoming impertinent again.

TYRTAEUS: Send me away, great Lord, if that's what you wish. I'll obey your brief command with equal brevity. The Spartan way. Because the reason you've trained your people to brevity of speech is so that, already, grammatically, you could annihilate the emergence of any judgment or criticism. The basic principle of your system is the wordless execution of a brief command. Everything rests upon a short principal sentence. Because it would be threatening for the regime to have even one subordinate clause that begins with 'but'. Command me to leave, great Lord, and I'll go, but the Spartan way of talking, which you consider so natural, is unnatural for me. I can only speak in my own way. My Lord, I doubt that brevity of speech contains much marrow. On the other hand, if I talk too much, you'll smash my brain marrow to a pulp. So what am I to do? My ears, nose and brain are in constant danger, and if all goes well, you'll also have my tongue cut out. I hope you understand my situation and will not have me blinded—leaving my lame leg as the only able part of me.

EUPATOR: What's the cause of your lameness? You didn't get that in battle? I can tell that it's a practiced, old lameness. Perhaps you can even run ...

TYRTAEUS: Run yes, but not run away.

EUPATOR: (*Flares up*) Was that hinting at our last retreat. Answer me!

TYRTAEUS: Must I answer that, great Lord?...

EUPATOR: Your question ... answered it. (*A brief silence*) Listen to me, lame one. I must know everything they say about Sparta. And I must know all the plans the enemy is making against us. I must have it because the decisive battle is near.

TYRTAEUS: I'm aware, great Lord. You're even conscripting the children.

EUPATOR: Yes, even the children. And if we have to, we'll even put spears into the hands of the newly born.

TYRTAEUS: Do you have to?

EUPATOR: We'll win, in spite of everything!

TYRTAEUS: What makes you think that, great Lord?

EUPATOR: Because we must win.

TYRTAEUS: Need is a mighty Lord. But the goddess of victory cannot be undressed by force; we must promise her something if we are to possess her. The poet writes poems to her. The sculptor makes a statue of her likeness, and the philosopher contemplates her flightiness. Only Sparta wants to rape her; because in Sparta you believe that the sole purpose of woman is to propagate.

EUPATOR: Talk to me about troop formations, lame one. Where are the Messenean positions? How many detachments are there? What are their weak points?

TYRTAEUS: I am a citizen of Messene, great Lord!

EUPATOR: You've already said that. Where do you plan to breach our lines? What are the plans of the Messenean supreme command? Where are they planning to have the crucial battle?

TYRTAEUS: I am a citizen of Messene great Lord, not a Spartan spy. Just an ordinary citizen of Messene, who has never yet looked into the playing cards of military commanders. I know neither the number of detachments, nor the time of the breakthrough, nor the planned site for the decisive battle. I only know one thing, great Lord, that Sparta has already lost this war.

EUPATOR: You're lying! We cannot lose this war because our very existence is at stake. The ancient mode of Spartan existence. Our ancestors are with us, they are our only allies. Whoever has Spartan blood flowing in his veins will fight so resolutely that only we can be victorious. Do you understand that, slave?!

TYRTAEUS: (*Softly*) My name is Tyrtaeus. I am a citizen of Messene.

EUPATOR: But over here, a slave. And by morning a dead slave. Vanish from my sight! (*He totters against the cloth wall of the tent where the map is*)

TYRTAEUS: Ephor, my heart pities you at least as much as my mind detests you. You are as cruel as the law, and as harsh as the cliffs of Taygetos. But the sledgehammer of Messene will pulverize you. As for my dying—I could've already died in battle or killed myself on the way here, knowing how slaves are dealt with in Sparta. Just one flawed step on the path along the cliffs, and instead of five slaves only four would've arrived here. You say that by morning I'll be dead. And if I leave now, that will surely be the case. Because no one will defend my cause before you. Yet I represent the cause of humanity, and you must hear me out.

EUPATOR: Your every word aims at the destruction of Sparta.

TYRTAEUS: Or wants to benefit it. Ask for peace, great Lord. Send ambassadors to Athens so that they can arrange peace for you. Promise them that among tribes who favor science and art, you will no longer be the drawn sword that threatens every statue or vase they create. Make plans for peace forthwith. Invite philosophers to Sparta, who will cogitate upon the salvation of its government and upon the laws of humanity. Think about peace, great Lord; for once, think about lasting peace. The reason Messene is fighting is to bring about peace, once and for all; even if it comes at the cost of the total annihilation of Sparta.

EUPATOR: How low have you sunk, Sparta, that a lame slave can say such things in front of one of your ephors.

TYRTAEUS: When can a person speak calmly, great Lord, if not when he knows that by morning he'll be dead. The thing that separates a human being from the cattle about to be slaughtered is that, before they kill him, he will at the very least try to reassure himself that his life had some meaning. You could have killed me already without my having been able to say anything. But now I am certain that my words won't remain without retribution. Therefore, I really can speak freely.

EUPATOR: (*After a slow sigh*) Well, speak then! It seems to me that you are not such an ordinary slave. There is something unusual about you. Or perhaps it is me. I have never yet spoken to slaves—nor would they have been allowed to speak in front of me. But now I feel uneasy in a way that I've never felt before. And yet, I yearn to know about things I never wanted to know about before.

TYRTAEUS: By morning you might also die. That's why you feel this way, ephor.

EUPATOR: There is equality in Sparta. A commander might die just as easily as a common soldier. With us, a commander is at the head of his troops not only in peace but also in battle.

TYRTAEUS: Equality is something entirely different, ephor.

EUPATOR: Everyone knows that there is equality in Sparta. Even you can't doubt that. Every citizen of Sparta has the right to vote, the size of everyone's plot of land is the same, food is common, and within certain constrains so are the women. What is that if not equality?!

TYRTAEUS: Is that what you call equality—that every man is to get equal fodder? Sage and fool equally at the feeding trough! Let's assume that it's right. But don't you have a single word to say about the slaves? When they are more numerous in Sparta than the Spartans?!

EUPATOR: But we have no Spartan-born slaves. Whoever's a slave is a foreigner.

TYRTAEUS: And aren't these foreigners the same as you? Don't they have the same mouth, nose and ears? Or do they have them just to confuse you, lest it should occur to you, in the name of Spartan equality, to cut off their noses and their ears.

EUPATOR: The slave is cattle—I do with him ...

TYRTAEUS: Whatever you want. I understand you, ephor. But think about what happens when a Spartan is taken prisoner. Then he's the one who's considered a slave in accordance with the laws of another land.

EUPATOR: A Spartan can never be a slave.

TYRTAEUS: Then how can a Messenean be one?

EUPATOR: Because the laws of Lycurgus prescribe it so.

TYRTAEUS: But the laws of Messene say other things.

EUPATOR: That's why we're at war.

TYRTAEUS: You want to decide in battle which country's laws are more just?

EUPATOR: Yes, because if we'll win, ours will be the one.

TYRTAEUS: Not that your laws are more just, only that you have the stronger army. A law that is just will never be found on the path of battle, ephor. A just law is very difficult to know. It's harder than defeating the enemy. Because in order for it to triumph, we must first triumph over ourselves. Tell me, great Lord, how does it benefit me if another has as many rights as I have? Of what benefit is it to me that I must always act in a considerate manner towards another; that I can't be uncontrolled or dissolute to another's detriment; that I cannot take what belongs to another, even though I'm the stronger; that I can't start a fight or a war just because another's grapevine is more lush than mine, his field more productive, or because there is a creek flowing at the back of his hill. How does it benefit me, great Lord, that I can't cut the other's throat before he's about to bite through mine; that I can't, like an animal, devour the defenseless; that I can't rob orphans of their inheritance or rape a lone woman? How does it benefit me, if I offer to carry the burden of the weary, or share my last bite with the hungry? None of these are of the least benefit to me. Isn't that so, great Lord? And still, the just law would say: "Share your last bite with the hungry and carry the burden of the weary. Let the lone woman pass in peace; give the orphans their part of the inheritance—always defend the defenseless. Don't ever cut the throat of another, because a battle can never rage between two truths—since a truth that brandishes a sword can no longer be a truth. The cause of truth cannot be fought over, it can only be defended. But even if you do defend it, don't ever imagine that it is a just cause to kill another in its name.

EUPATOR: The things you say are full of contradictions ...

TYRTAEUS: It only seems that way. Because perfect truth doesn't exist for us humans, because we are not perfect. Human truth is in the same ratio to the absolute as humans are to perfection. Consequently, the closer a human being is to perfection, the more just are his laws. Every human being comes into the world as an inheritor of a great wealth, which is the truth. And throughout his life, he'll need to apportion this inheritance into smaller valuables that represent his rights. If you recognize human rights but apply them only to a small circle, shutting out all others, you are committing an injustice, and your laws will be as far from the truth as is the distance that separates justice from injustice. If you give rights only to a few, you haven't achieved justice. If you give rights equally to everyone, then you'll be just. In the hands of a single individual, only the sum total of the rights due to him guarantees natural law, which is the right of every human being. A person's rights will only turn into natural law if they contain as many shares of the truth as are his, in accordance with his individual nature. More for the wise, less for the foolish. Among the animals, natural right belongs to the stronger. But since we are not animals, the right of the stronger is not natural for us. Those who are weakest in battle, the ones who were not born for boxing; whom you put upon the cliffs of Taygetos are often the best thinkers. That's why there are no poets, sculptors and philosophers amongst you. Because you've always stood by the rights of the stronger which, from the point of view of humankind, represents injustice. That's why Sparta's truth is not the truth. And since you cannot defend it with the mind, you defend it with the fist. Spartan law is the law of the fist, my Lord.

EUPATOR: So what does justice mean according to you.

TYRTAEUS: Justice, great Lord, is a condition in which everyone can do what anyone else can do, and no one has to endure what he himself mustn't commit.

EUPATOR: This is in keeping with the spirit of Spartan equality.

TYRTAEUS: But it is not in keeping with what Spartan equality maintains towards the slaves.

EUPATOR: You believe that everyone's equal?

TYRTAEUS: Yes. But equality doesn't mean that the same number of benefits are due to every human being. Only the foolish can believe that. And the more foolish one is, the more one wishes that it be so. The right to education, for instance, means that every human being, rich or poor, must be given the opportunity to be educated, but it doesn't mean that every one will become a scholar. Each according to his capabilities. Only our rights are equal, my Lord; not the diligence or talent with which we realize those rights. An outstanding person will be living within a broader circle of rights than those who are spiritually henpecked. But no one, not even the wisest, can ever obtain the right to commit injustice against the ignorant. The coups d'état are frequently committed by those who are excluded from the frontline, not because of rights but because of lack of talent. Yet even you would grant that leadership in government belongs to those who can fill natural law with substance. It is the scholars, sages, poets and inventors who enlarge natural law for all human beings. The right of leadership in government therefore belongs to them and not to the rabble, for whom equality means that no one should have more than those who can't and don't even want to live with their portion of natural law. The rights of every human being are equal, but the licenses brought about by the realization of these rights are not equal.

EUPATOR: According to this, you'd even oppose the general right to vote. Yet, that also exists in Sparta.

TYRTAEUS: Yes, my Lord. Because the right to vote can be a very dangerous tool in the hands of a clever demagogue and a lot of ignorant and foolish voters. The right to vote doesn't just mean that one can decide over his own fate, it also means that one can decide the fate of those who are cognizant. In any case, the right to vote is not the kind that springs from natural law, but rather from human nature, since it regulates living together. People will often give power to those who appeal to their feelings and not to reason. You yourself said, just a short while ago, that whoever has Spartan blood flowing in his veins will fight resolutely, instead of saying that they'll fight because they are convinced of the rightness of the Spartan way of life. I'd therefore make the right to vote subject to an examination, so that decision making would only belong to those who know what that right means.

EUPATOR: The teacher in you shows himself at last.

TYRTAEUS: I know that's what you're most afraid of. Because, look, a lame teacher whom you regard as a hated Messenean slave, comes over here and speaks to you about the truth, and you, a leader of Sparta, immediately detects teaching in his words. That's what frightens you the most and that's why you're fighting against Messene, lest any such teaching should be listened to by one Spartan, ten Spartans and then a hundred Spartans. And you are scared that in the end the whole of Sparta will be leaning towards it.

EUPATOR: A person who's clever with words can easily push a soldier into a corner.

TYRTAEUS: But you're not just a soldier, ephor, you are a statesman as well. And I heard it said that you've composed more than one battle hymn for Sparta.

EUPATOR: That was when I was still young.

TYRTAEUS: Ephor, one should never be ashamed of the resolute melodies of youth. Do you remember any of them?

EUPATOR: There now, teacher, we've progressed to the singing lesson.

TYRTAEUS: Earlier on, when your son, with clenched teeth, thrashed around in agony, you were as hard as a statue because you were being watched. But now we don't have to pretend in front of one other. Won't you sing one of them to me.

EUPATOR: But I am not a singer, and I don't remember a single one any more. They were foolish nothings. I will confess, though, that in the beginning they were not even fighting hymns ... but songs of love. Then my father made me understand that it cannot be. That I must be tough because I'm a Spartan. So I changed their wording and their melody here and there, and they became battle hymns. Battle hymns from verses of love. Because over here, the millet is sparser than anywhere else. And if we cannot guard it with the toughest fists, then even the little we have will be taken from us by those who outnumber us. And so our sole concern must be with fighting. We've got to be tougher than the others because we are fewer, even though we are still too many for the millet that's ours. What are ... surely you're not crying ...

your eyes seem suspiciously shiny.

TYRTAEUS: I am not crying, ephor, I am just moved by how little we humans know each other. The most bloodthirsty beasts of the forest don't have a reputation worse than yours, ephor Eupator. You are the very model of toughness.

EUPATOR: It's difficult to be so tough, Tyrtaeus; difficult to make our lives as rigid as the law of life demands it. But since it demands it, I do it, and so do many more Spartans along with me. Lycurgus gave us our laws, and be they good or bad, if they were good enough for our glorious ancestors, then they have to be good enough for us as well. You accuse us of being merciless with the slaves, even though they are more numerous in Sparta than the Spartans. You should hear what yours are doing with captives from Sparta. They cut pockets into their bellies and stuff them with their lower arms, which they've cut off at the elbow.

TYRTAEUS: It is horrible to hear such things.

EUPATOR: Well, that's how your democrats fight.

TYRTAEUS: My Lord, this war is already degenerate; monstrous things occur on both sides—but a cause cannot be made synonymous with an atrocity.

EUPATOR: So you do admit that you were the ones who started with hacking off limbs.

TYRTAEUS: No commander, you did, at the swamp of Parthos.

EUPATOR: Even before that. We found limbless corpses at Limon. Afterwards, we brought them home and buried them with dignity.

TYRTAEUS: Sure. Except that those were the limbless corpses of Messenean soldiers, whom you buried with dignity in order to continue whipping up the sentiments of the population here in Sparta.

EUPATOR: Don't argue, slave.

TYRTAEUS: If I were a fighter instead of a captive, one of us would be knocked out now.

EUPATOR: (*Bursts out laughing*) I don't mean harm, Tyrtaeus, but you look ridiculous in this fighting mode—like a lame rooster. Let's stop hurting each other because there's no way that we'll be able to clarify the issue of responsibility in war. Because victory is not enough for the victor; he needs moral reasons to justify his right to victory. We are compelled to fight you because we cannot share the little we have; and since your numbers continue to increase around us, we can't wait until you'll turn into a decisive majority. We are attacking for reasons of national defense.

TYRTAEUS: Just so you can defend a mendacious order.

EUPATOR: And what sends you into battle? There is a handful of idealists among you who can't see past their noses, and consequently believe that they're fighting for ideals that they should also inject into our people; whereas in reality there are just a few landowners, merchants and shipping magnates who direct your activities.

TYRTAEUS: Ephor, we are fighting for freedom. We want to make every human being free.

EUPATOR: So, is everyone free over there? Can the poor do exactly the same as the rich? First give your own people freedom. Then subjugate mine, so that they can be just as free as the proletariat is in your country. The things you say are beautiful, but they cannot be realized. The population needs bread, always more bread. And there's no great art in conquering more and more countries in order to give it to them. But to give less bread to more people, accustoming them to a lifestyle that will not make them rebel—that's an achievement, my lame dreamer. To give them less not just for a year, but for decades—throughout a lifetime. You can only do that with the kind of people who carry relinquishment in their blood; and who, rather than sinking into the ocean of peoples, for the sake of maintaining their national identity, relinquish everything that the rich nations consider the meaning of life. It's easy to write sarcastic verse ridiculing the fact that we go around almost naked. But what are we to do if we have even more need of grain than of cloth. So we wrap ourselves in rags. It's hard for a people that doesn't collect treasures, because no matter what treasure came into its hands, it wouldn't get anything for it. We guard the laws of our ancestors, and train ourselves all our lives to make do with little. With so little that what was enough for our ancestors is also enough for their prolific descendants. We need to fight because any excess in our population must perish. Such a nation can be accused of being merciless with its slaves, but why would it be tolerant with them if it isn't tolerant with its own.

TYRTAEUS: You offer new points of view, ephor—that much is true.

EUPATOR: When you entered my tent, Tyrtaeus, I saw how you searched it with your eyes, looking for a picture, a statue or a vase that would soften the barrenness of these grey walls. Do you really believe that it doesn't bother me to lie naked on rough matting, or that I have grown so used to the taste of millet that I don't yearn for anything else? But why should I relinquish my ancestors and their way of life? What is that guiding ideal that would unite Sparta and Messene? You hold your laws to be true, and we believe the same about ours. And you, Tyrtaeus, who are a Messenean, don't represent the laws of Messene; but the tenets of a few honorable philosophers. Yet even you must admit that a country cannot be exchanged for such a fiction, no matter how right it appears. There are times when I too think that there should be something that unites the many small city-states that are constantly fighting with each other. After all, our gods are the same, and we seem to get along with each other in the stadium as well. But then, when I hear that once again Messene harvested our fruit trees along the border, anger and worry compels me to bash a few Messeneans on the head.

Are you listening, son? Even you must admit that philosophy isn't everything. On the other hand, a bit of it does no harm, especially in the mind of a kid as stubbornly Spartan as Demetrios. So take on his tutoring, Tyrtaeus, until he recovers from his injury. Teach him all manner of learning, since nothing will make an impression on him anyway. Talk to him about your philosophical beliefs and teach him melodies so that he'll have something to forget the first time his sword runs through the heart of a terror-stricken Messenean.

ACT II

SCENE 1

Upstage, a rocky hillside covered with flowers. Stage right, there are several bushes. Olive trees are in the center of the stage. Downstage on both sides is a clearing covered by grass. From the stage left, wearing a cloak, Tyrtaeus enters with Demetrios.

TYRTAEUS: Demetrios, go pick some flowers.

DEMETRIOS: Flowers? Teacher, whatever for? They're good for nothing. I'd rather rest my bad leg, it really hurts here in the bend.

TYRTAEUS: Go, pick some flowers, son.

DEMETRIOS: You have some strange ideas. Why should I pick flowers when every flower that grows in Sparta is ours. I'd rather rest my leg. It really hurts.

TYRTAEUS: Do you mean that flowers are ours in the same way that everything is communal in Sparta? But that's how you used to talk about the pathways of the stars as well. Remember how you asked me what the sense was of observing their journey given that they're there anyway whether we watch them or not? But when the starry sky opened its secrets to you, you realized that the particular characteristics of stars should be observed because there's a connection between their journey and our fate. You'll get to think about flowers in the same way. They are not there merely for the sake of our nodding recognition as we pass by the violet, snapdragon, marigold and the others. Flowers also have lives. They have characteristics, species and gender. Nature has its own order. Bring me a bunch of flowers, and we'll make some comparisons.

DEMETRIOS: But my leg ...

TYRTAEUS: It'll do your leg good as well. You must exercise it and make it strong. If you sit or lie around too much you could stay lame forever.

DEMETRIOS: If only you hadn't said that master. All right. I'll rather study the weeds. (*He goes out on stage right behind the bushes. Laughing, Tyrtaeus follows him with his eyes. He spreads his cloak at the base of an olive tree and sits down. A song is heard in the distance. Upstage left, it's coming closer and closer. Tyrtaeus leans forward and looks in the direction of the singing. Photina appears carrying a large bundle of firewood*)

TYRTAEUS: My good woman, why are you carrying firewood instead of picking flowers?

PHOTINA: (*Taken aback*) What kind of talk is that, stranger? Let me pass. I'm the spouse of a Spartan fighter.

TYRTAEUS: (*Stands up*) I didn't want to block your way. I asked only because I'm curious about every peculiarity that exists in Sparta.

PHOTINA: So you're not only a stranger, you're also a stranger in Sparta.

TYRTAEUS: I'm not only a foreigner, I'm the enemy as well.

PHOTINA: So you're a slave.

TYRTAEUS: A Spartan answer. Since over here the enemy can only be a slave. You people know nothing about conventions for prisoners of war. (*Mostly to himself*) But if peace were to come, the slaves would be freed.

PHOTINA: But that's why we're at war, to get more slaves? Some people must be working in the fields!

TYRTAEUS: What do the men do in Sparta?

PHOTINA: (*With a somewhat stupid haughtiness*) A Spartan man cannot do the work of slaves. His task is to train himself for battle.

TYRTAEUS: I understand. He trains for battle, so he won't have to work.

PHOTINA: Say that again?

TYRTAEUS: Why should I? You'd only take it amiss ... Be on your way. You're the spouse of a Spartan fighter, and I am only a slave.

PHOTINA: I'm going. I'm going. (*She sits down*)

TYRTAEUS: Oh, so you are not only a spouse, but a mother-to-be as well.

PHOTINA: (*With proud joy*) You've noticed. So don't you dare badmouth Spartan men to me.

TYRTAEUS: Since I cannot praise them, I'd rather go. (*He takes two steps*)

PHOTINA: Look at that! You're lame.

TYRTAEUS: (*Hurt*) So what?

PHOTINA: (*With childish enthusiasm*) Please, stay. I have never seen a lame person before.

TYRTAEUS: (*Still hurt*) And does it appeal to you?

PHOTINA: You bet! You know, in Sparta there is not a single person who is lame.

TYRTAEUS: What about the war-wounded?

PHOTINA: That's different. They're Spartan heroes who received their wounds for the fatherland. But a lame slave! That's like a barren cow. It has no use.

TYRTAEUS: So you think that all slaves belong in the fields. Then I have nothing to talk to you about. May the gods be with you.

PHOTINA: Don't go. Or rather, go, but just a few steps. Your limping is so amusing. You know, when I give birth to this child I'd like to tell him about it, so that he in turn can tell his grandchildren: "Before I was born, my mother saw a lame slave."

TYRTAEUS: (*Cruelly*) You too could be giving birth to a lame son.

PHOTINA: May the gods protect me from that. You know what would happen to him ...

TYRTAEUS: If that thought torments you, then you shouldn't be tormenting me with it.

PHOTINA: Are you angry?

TYRTAEUS: Can a slave be angry with the spouse of a Spartan fighter?

PHOTINA: Then take a few steps. I'm asking you. I'm asking you very nicely. I want so much to see it. And if a woman in my condition desires something, then she should have it.

TYRTAEUS: (*Unwillingly, he takes a few steps then says cruelly*) There!

PHOTINA: (*Claps with delight*) You know slave, it is more interesting than a Spartan ceremonial parade. Go on. (*Very reluctantly, he takes a few more steps*) But limp harder! Don't try to hide it. (*He takes a couple more steps*) There. That's better. You walk just like lame dogs do.

TYRTAEUS: (*Deeply hurt*) I've had enough ... I'm going. (*He stops*) I just want to say ...

PHOTINA: You know what, come, sit down, then I don't have to think about you being lame. (*Tyrtaeus pauses. Photina pats the grass in invitation. Tyrtaeus slowly sits down at a distance from Photina*)

PHOTINA: There, you see, this way neither of us looks flawed.

TYRTAEUS: A woman and a man who only count from the waist up.

PHOTINA: You talk so strangely. What do you mean by a man and a woman ... and I still don't understand what you said earlier, though there is something to it.

TYRTAEUS: I said many things. What are you referring to?

PHOTINA: Well, that the men fight so they won't have to work. Is that how it is everywhere?

TYRTAEUS: If everywhere else was the same as it is in Sparta, no one would fight against you. The reason you want to destroy others is because their ways are different. And that's why they want to annihilate you.

PHOTINA: But isn't it true that everything here is how it should be, as the great Lycurgus decreed?

TYRTAEUS: Well, then you're sinning by being curious.

PHOTINA: I only want to sin a little bit, and I command you, slave, not to tell anyone about it. I am curious. So speak. In my condition ...

TYRTAEUS: I suspect that these things would interest you even if you weren't in your condition.

PHOTINA: You're being insolent, slave, and you're abusing the fact that we're alone.

TYRTAEUS: If a man and a woman are alone, yet are sitting this far away from each other, then they are truly abusing the situation.

PHOTINA: You keep talking about strange things in a strange way ... It churns me up. Why are you using words like ...

TYRTAEUS: ... like ...

PHOTINA: I can't even explain it. But you're different from the slaves who pull the yoke in the fields. They are truly ...

TYRTAEUS: ... slaves ... Is that what you wanted to say? It is possible that I'm different from them. That would have to do with the fact that I was also a different kind of person in a country where these slaves were free men.

PHOTINA: So what are you?

TYRTAEUS: I'm a poet!

PHOTINA: And what's that?

TYRTAEUS: A poet is the kind of person who does what he shouldn't do and doesn't do what he should do. But you wouldn't understand that.

PHOTINA: But I do understand it! (*Triumphantly*) Because I am also a poet!

TYRTAEUS: How's that?

PHOTINA: Well, here I am speaking to you, when I shouldn't be speaking to you, and although I should leave you, I'm staying.

TYRTAEUS: What would the great Lycurgus say to this?

PHOTINA: I don't know. Don't you have a Lycurgus where you come from?

TYRTAEUS: No.

PHOTINA: But then, who makes your laws?

TYRTAEUS: We make them ourselves.

PHOTINA: You too?

TYRTAEUS: Yes, me too.

PHOTINA: Then you are also a little bit of a Lycurgus.

TYRTAEUS: Yes, where I come from, every person counts as the most important a little bit—because we are all involved in making decisions about our future.

PHOTINA: Well, that's all right then. You could even argue with Lycurgus. Since you've also created laws. Tell me more, I'm listening.

TYRTAEUS: And I am listening to you. You have such a beautiful voice.

PHOTINA: What did you say I have?

TYRTAEUS: A beautiful voice.

PHOTINA: My voice is not beautiful. I was never able to command because of it. In running, jumping, discus-throwing, I was always the first. But my voice let me down. It could barely be heard ten paces away from me ... it was too soft.

TYRTAEUS: That's just it. Your voice is as soft as the sound of a Euboean flute.

PHOTINA: What manner of speech is this?

TYRTAEUS: Was I improper again?

PHOTINA: No, that's not it. But you speak to me as if I were sick.

TYRTAEUS: Where I come from, women are always spoken to that way.

PHOTINA: Perhaps they are always sick?

TYRTAEUS: No. That is to say, not in the way you think. But they are often lovesick.

PHOTINA: What kind of a sickness is that?

TYRTAEUS: Love is the kind of sickness for which women forgive the men who made them sick.

PHOTINA: You keep on churning me up inside. Why do women and men bother with each other so much where you come from? Do your women run faster than the men?

TYRTAEUS: No.

PHOTINA: Are they stronger?

TYRTAEUS: Yes, but not in the way you think.

PHOTINA: Do they go to battle?

TYRTAEUS: That's not it.

PHOTINA: Then I don't get it.

TYRTAEUS: What don't you get?

PHOTINA: I don't even understand that. You talk about women as if they are more important than men.

TYRTAEUS: Not more important, perhaps just better. Where I come from, women are important not because of what they do, but because we consider them so.

PHOTINA: And why would the men want it to be like that? Over here, the men don't want women to have any importance whatsoever. That's why we do our exercises naked in front of them, so they can prove to themselves that it has no significance whatsoever.

TYRTAEUS: And that's why, in the dead of night, shamefaced and stealthy like a thief, they scurry into the tent of anyone among you who doesn't have a child; just so that they can liken the whole business to the process of digestion. It isn't like that with us. A man feels proud if a woman has spent the night with him. The poets write poems about great love and recite them everywhere, and just hearing it brings tears to the eyes of the audience. Where I come from, love is a free and sacred thing. But you doubtless prefer it the Spartan way, since the one and only, unappealable, great Lycurgus commanded it thus: Let the women cook the soup and give birth to children.

PHOTINA: (*Startled, she puts her arm around the bunch of sticks and attempts to stand up*) I have to go to cook soup ...

TYRTAEUS: And give birth to your child ... So go! (*Photina stays sitting where she is*)

PHOTINA: I don't understand it. We keep on saying that we'll go, yet neither of us moves. What is it that brought us together like this?

TYRTAEUS: I have no idea what brought us together, but one thing's for sure, if either of us suggests moving closer, the other would have to go.

PHOTINA: That much I do understand! Isn't it curious how the things I do or don't understand run contrary to your expectations. Why is that?

TYRTAEUS: Because the soul of a woman is much more refined than the soul of a man. Women instinctively grasp things that men seem incapable of comprehending. Generally speaking, men are only capable of being incapable.

PHOTINA: (*Laughs*) Perhaps you don't think of yourself as a man, given the way you carry on about man.

TYRTAEUS: One can discuss men and praise women. But love merits silence. (*Pause*) Why are you silent?

PHOTINA: Because I'm sick, and I would like you to talk to me as if you'd also caught it. Tell me your name. Mine is Photina.

TYRTAEUS: Tyrtaeus.

PHOTINA: Do other women call you that?

TYRTAEUS: It's my name, Photina.

PHOTINA: I don't like sharing with other women. Anyway, that's a Spartan name.

TYRTAEUS: Then for the sake of my name, I'll be Spartan too. Would you like that?

PHOTINA: You are lame, you can never be a Spartan. And I'll be giving birth to a child whose father is a Spartan.

TYRTAEUS: Why are you hurting me?

PHOTINA: Because I want you to be sick. To feel the same pain that I'm feeling in here (*puts her hand to her chest*) That is the only thing possible between us.

TYRTAEUS: Who can tell what's possible ...

PHOTINA: Don't be sad! When I give birth to this child I will think that you are his father. Since my husband was only good for what Lycurgus decreed for me. Everything else I learned from a lame slave.

TYRTAEUS: Are you saying that I'll be the soul-father of your child?

PHOTINA: Of my child and of my dreams.

TYRTAEUS: So you do dream? I thought that was also forbidden in Sparta. Lycurgus is so circumspect. Perhaps you've even dreamt about being alive. That you are alive, but not here in Sparta.

PHOTINA: Now you are the one who's hurting me.

TYRTAEUS: You tell me that I can never be a Spartan because I'm lame; and I'm telling you that in your dreams, you long for Athens. It shows that you can only hurt the other by touching the pain here, inside. (*He gestures towards his heart*) You are dreaming about Athens, Photina—about its harbor and the ocean, about slender sails and precious pearls. You're dreaming about Athens, but you'll be giving birth to a son of Sparta. Why don't you give birth to the son of your dreams?

PHOTINA: Why can't my dreams make me fertile? Why is a man's greedy loin a greater reality than what a woman expects from life?

TYRTAEUS: Are there many women in Sparta who feel as you do?

PHOTINA: I don't know. But I've just understood that over here women bring their sons into the world for Sparta and not for themselves.

TYRTAEUS: So now you can see it. There's no joy in Sparta, only compulsion. You'll be giving birth to a child out of compulsion. Such is the living blood tax of Sparta.

PHOTINA: How I hate my own womb now, and the birth pains I'll have to endure without rejoicing.

TYRTAEUS: Your words, Photina, not mine. Yet I could tell you stories about women who are singing as they gather flowers instead of firewood. Women whose goal in life is hardly more than to preserve their beauty as long as possible. How they use perfumed oils and delicate paints to heighten their charms for their man. I could tell you about the jewels many of them receive, because their husbands hold them to be more precious than the finest gems. And I could tell you about soft, delicate music and about great joy. But for you, the law prescribes three things: cook the soup, give birth and honor Lycurgus above all.

PHOTINA: You are lame, so you can never be a Spartan. But for me it is still possible not to be one.

TYRTAEUS: Anger has taken you far, Photina, but you must know that the rest of the world is not quite as you imagine it. That would only be true if it were according to your dreams and not as it is in reality. The world outside only promises those things that you hope to receive from it so promptly. Over there, everything is freely available, but what's the good of it if you can't afford to pay for it? In Sparta, there are neither rich nor poor. It's the external constraints that rob all of you equally of happiness. But needing to put internal constraints upon oneself can make life just as bleak—when you realize that others, who, same as you, were given birth by a mother, steal all the pleasures from you. And in proportion to your nothing, their advantage is over a hundred fold.

PHOTINA: It seems as if we might as well end up on the cliffs of

Taygetos. Oh, how terrible this is. Happiness is all around us, even nature wants it that way. And then contemptible power mongers surround it with guarded fences so that we can never get near it.

TYRTAEUS: That's how it is, Photina.

PHOTINA: Isn't there anyone who would want to change it?

TYRTAEUS: There is, Photina!

PHOTINA: You, Tyrtaeus? The whole world against a lame one.

TYRTAEUS: A lame one against a world that is limping. It's a much smaller task if one looks at it that way. When I left Messene, I harbored such hatred against Sparta that it blinded me to seeing the flaws of the world in which I lived. I marched against all of Sparta, but now I realize that we just need to fight against its laws, not its existence. And everything I've experienced convinces me that the more sins there are, the fewer the shoulders upon which the responsibility rests. So don't hate your child, Photina, because a better world still has to come with those who have not yet been born.

PHOTINA: Someone else is needed here, Tyrtaeus, not you. Someone who accomplishes things by hook or by crook, and rids us of the evil ones. Someone in whom hatred has gone so far out of control that it obscures any nobility of mind. Because I know there are some sins compared to which the only greater sin is if we don't commit them.

TYRTAEUS: Your words terrify me, Photina. Sin can never be so noble that it could be turned into a virtue.

PHOTINA: You live in the clouds, Tyrtaeus. You want something and you want its antithesis as well. You herald hatred, and love emanates from your words. You brandish the whip and it descends like a caress. At times your gestures look as if you are waving to the olive trees. You seem to greet them as a person returning from far away would greet his loved ones. (*Pause*) Tell me, were you born lame?

TYRTAEUS: Yes, Photina.

PHOTINA: If you hadn't said that, I'd have thought that you're a Spartan. You talk like a thief who, as a child, was taken far from his parental home, and now upon his return would like to rob the grave of his rich parents. But in the last moment he stops in his tracks because these were his parents after all, and so he'd rather utter a prayer at their grave. And yet what a rich inheritance would await the one who destroyed Sparta.

TYRTAEUS: One needs to change it, Photina, not destroy it. Tell me, would you betray your country to obtain satisfaction for your own truth?

PHOTINA: I don't know what I would do, because I know no other country than Sparta.

TYRTAEUS: For you, it isn't just your country, it's the whole world.

PHOTINA: For me, the whole world is what Sparta is missing from. Tyrtaeus, you're hiding something from me?

TYRTAEUS: I only have one secret —that of being lame. I've just realized that my whole soul is tied to my lameness. It allows me neither to fall nor to fly. How can it be that others don't recognize you as a whole person!

PHOTINA: Such self-doubt will get you into trouble. You'll err with the decisive step.

TYRTAEUS: This isn't doubting. It's destiny itself.

PHOTINA: What are you talking about?

TYRTAEUS: I am talking about something that I haven't dared to discuss even with myself. Whether I would have become the person I am today if I hadn't been born lame. Would I have turned into the kind of soldier who, along with thousands of others, goes into battle? Would I ever have doubted? Would I have questioned the laws of humanity?

PHOTINA: Don't think about what would've happened then. You are the person you've become.

TYRTAEUS: But am I really that person? Believe me, there are times when I would give all my knowledge just to hear the clinking of an able-bodied soldier's armor on me.

PHOTINA: Do not torment yourself with such foolishness.

TYRTAEUS: But it isn't foolishness. I must know who I really am. And whether I'm capable of a truly worthy task. Whether something that others wouldn't undertake with an able body, would not prove to be too much for someone with a disability. Because that is my truth, I have a disability. Oh, what is the worth of a striving soul when every street urchin yells after you and mocks you? When women laugh at you behind your back? What is the worth of a good mind when my eyes fill with tears if I see a statue with perfect muscles. Oh, what I wouldn't give, Photina, if I could accomplish a task which is given to an able-bodied person. Who knows that I wouldn't give everything I am for it, including my soul. Help me, Photina ... come closer ...

PHOTINA: "Should either of us suggest moving closer, the other would definitely have to go." You were the one who said it, Tyrtaeus. Dying and decision making can only be done in person. I'm leaving now because I know that the further I get from you, the closer I'll be to our dreams.

DEMETRIOS: (*Comes with an armful of flowers*) Look, teacher, what a lot of flowers I picked for us. Ah, Photina, your belly is getting bigger. Are you sure you're not carrying firewood in there as well?

TYRTAEUS: Be quiet, Demetrios. Bring the flowers here. (*He takes the flowers, and slowly spreads them at Photina's feet*)

DEMETRIOS: (*With indignation*) But you told me that we're going to study the flowers.

TYRTAEUS: One can learn about them much better if they've been touched by the feet of a woman. (*Photina departs slowly*)

DEMETRIOS: (*After a short pause*) It seems to me that you've been studying something else.

TYRTAEUS: (*Startled, he moves his gaze from the disappearing Photina*) You are right, Demetrios. Let us continue our studies.

DEMETRIOS: I'd rather be fencing. This business of picking flowers really did help my leg.

TYRTAEUS: (*The idea grabs hold of him*) Would you fence with me? I could hardly be your teacher where that is concerned.

DEMETRIOS: I'll teach you. Fencing is tremendously manly.

TYRTAEUS: Do you think it's possible to fence with a lame leg?

DEMETRIOS: We'll fence without shifting position. I'll give you a good thrashing.

TYRTAEUS: Take care, Demetrios, that I don't surprise you.

DEMETRIOS: Don't you worry. I've even thrashed the fencing master. Giving someone a thorough thrashing is worth as much as the theory of Pythagoras.

TYRTAEUS: And a lot of ignorant boys have been thrashed for not knowing it.

DEMETRIOS: Look, teacher, those two branches are just made for it. I'll get them for us. (*He takes them from one of the olive trees*) There you are. Let's begin. (*He bows as fencing adversaries do*)

TYRTAEUS: Take care you don't poke my eyes out.

DEMETRIOS: You take care that I don't. Because I want to poke them out. (*They thrash each other. Eupator comes from stage left. He is carrying a rolled-up scroll in one hand*)

EUPATOR: Well, if it isn't the pupil instructing the teacher.

TYRTAEUS: Honor to you, ephor Eupator!

EUPATOR: Let's hope you're doing as well with your other studies.

DEMETRIOS: Look, father, this is the greatest wisdom; holding a bludgeon in the palm of your hand.

TYRTAEUS: A good teacher must know about this as well, my Lord, since the only thing mightier than the power of philosophy is the philosophy of power. Only temporarily of course. Philosophy always wins out in the end. Contemplation precedes, overtakes and leaves the deed behind.

EUPATOR: (*Somberly*) But sometimes a fact goes beyond anything that we could possibly contemplate.

TYRTAEUS: Is there bad news, ephor?

EUPATOR: Demetrios, go and wait for us in my tent.

DEMETRIOS: Yes, father, I'll just take these. (*He takes from Tyrtaeus the branch he used for fencing*) We might need them. (*He leaves*)

EUPATOR: (*To himself*) Yes, pretty soon Sparta will need every stick there is. I hope it gives you pleasure, Tyrtaeus.

TYRTAEUS: I couldn't give you an account of my feelings right now. But are you able to tell me what's happening, or is it a state secret?

EUPATOR: More like a nation's shame. Tyrtaeus, you come and go in our homeland with open eyes. You know that the string is stretched to the utmost. But now we're at a stage where Sparta's very existence could easily be crushed from one day to the next.

TYRTAEUS: And the prophecy of Delphi?

EUPATOR: As you know, the prophecy said: "Ask Athens for a leader who will carry your fight to victory."

TYRTAEUS: And did you send the emissaries to Athens?

EUPATOR: They've already come back.

TYRTAEUS: With a leader?

EUPATOR: Instead of a leader, another message. (*He unrolls the scroll and reads from it*)

> Where muscle and strength have been to no avail
> the lame, the paralytic or the blind may help.
> Above all, the commander's to be brainy,
> his soul's to be on fire
> and his tongue be clever with words.

SCENE 2

In Eupator's tent, as in Act I, Scene 1. The five ephors are conferring together.

NOSOS: Did you ask me here to lecture me? I know what I have to do. I am the commander.

EUPATOR: Nosos, you may be the commander, but you must realize that it can't continue this way.

NOSOS: Is it my fault or yours?

TINOS: And just why would it be our fault?

NOSOS: Is it your laurel that makes you talk so boldly?

TINOS: I wasn't even thinking of it. But since you mention it, I did win it for Sparta.

NOSOS: (*With contempt*) In running.

TINOS: You, on the other hand, didn't win a laurel in anything, and right now you are being chased by the enemy. You won't win a laurel for that either.

NOSOS: You better watch how you talk to me!

TINOS: It's you who had better watch over Sparta!

NOSOS: Am I a sentry or the commander?

TINOS: We'd be better off if we had picked a common sentry for a commander. Anyone could have done better.

PATON: Why are you killing each other with words, when only action will help us now.

TINOS: Or another commander.

PHYLO: Noble ephors, I want to be impartial amongst you. Isn't there a common formula we could all agree to?

EUPATOR: There is only one formula: victory!

PATON: We are all in agreement there.

TINOS: Victory at all cost and regardless of who stands in its way.

NOSOS: Is it me you're talking about? Is there anyone in the whole of Sparta more suited to my rank than I am?

TINOS: We know from the gods that there is!

NOSOS: From the ...?

EUPATOR: Yes, commander. It was our joint decision, but we didn't do it behind your back. We were just unable to get word to you. Despair goaded us to it. Because the enemy is already at the gates of Sparta.

NOSOS: Oh, this is wicked. The doubt is in you, and so you're doubting me. Had you as much faith in the spirit of the ancients as I do, your belief in the invincibility of Sparta would also be rock solid. And you'd know that since Sparta has never yet been defeated, it couldn't possibly be defeated now.

TINOS: It has never been defeated, it can't possibly be defeated; so why are we faring so disastrously now.

NOSOS: Battles might be lost, but the final victory will be ours.

TINOS: Perhaps, if the commander at the head of our army is

pleasing to the gods.

NOSOS: I see that you've already conspired against me. My god is Sparta. I believe in it against all other gods.

PHYLO: Please, don't speak so loudly. (*He points upwards*) They might hear it.

EUPATOR: We've been in similar predicaments before. But the gods have always helped us. That's why we turned again to Delphi, so that we could find out their wishes.

NOSOS: (*Contemptuously*) And what did the gods tell you?

EUPATOR: That we should ask Athens for a commander.

NOSOS: Athens? (*Sarcastically*) A merchant perhaps? Who in exchange for some shimmering cloth will purchase our victory from Messene?

PATON: The gods said to ask Athens for a commander ...

PHYLO: And humbled as I was, I was brave enough to lead emissaries to Athens to bring back a commander.

NOSOS: (*As above*) And did you bring one back?

PHYLO: Instead of a commander this is what we got. (*He takes out the scroll and lets it unfurl*)

NOSOS: A scroll? Can insolence against Sparta go without retribution?

TINOS: Better a commander from a scroll than one who can't even read from it.

NOSOS: Yes, I know. That's where the fault lies. That's why I'm not good enough for you because I am ancient Sparta itself. And there aren't ten new things I would exchange for a single one of the old ones.

EUPATOR: We honor you, Nosos, commander and ephor. But we love Sparta more—to live with your own words—than to allow anyone to come before it.

PATON: A whole nation cannot be allowed to go to ruin just because of the feelings of one person. You must understand that.

NOSOS: I do understand it. You can't use a sword against me, so you ambush me with clever words. What does the prophecy say?

PHYLO: Now you're talking. We can work this out together.

Ephor Eupator, please read it.

EUPATOR: With your permission, commander Nosos, because we would always leave you with your title.

PHYLO: We can have two commanders, can't we?

PATON: The priority is victory. Surely, we are all in agreement on that.

NOSOS: Read what the message says.

PHYLO: The message is somewhat obscure. So let us give all our attention to it. Attention is akin to discipline. (*He gives an awkward laugh. Suddenly Eupator starts reading*)

EUPATOR: Where muscle and strength have been to no avail
the lame, the paralytic or the blind may help.
Above all, the commander's to be brainy,
his soul's to be on fire
and his tongue be clever with words.

NOSOS: (*Shaken*) Read it again. Perhaps I understood it wrong. (*Eupator reads it once more slowly, enunciating every syllable*)

NOSOS: (*Fighting with himself*) You, have you all read this before?

PHYLO: We were brave enough to read it, to study it, and even to argue about its hidden meaning.

NOSOS: (*Almost weeping, cries out in consternation*) You argued over such impertinence? Instead of throwing it into the fire?

PHYLO: (*Shocked*) What are you saying! To throw the will of the gods into the fire?

NOSOS: The gods can't possibly be wanting such a disgrace. That a cripple should command Sparta! Swear upon the gods that this can never be!

PATON: How could we swear to such a thing when it would mean swearing against their express wishes?

NOSOS: Then do so. Better than to endure such infamy.

EUPATOR: Come to your senses, Nosos. We asked the gods for their protection. To go against their wishes would mean certain ruin.

NOSOS: Then let the gods perish if they want to destroy us. Let us freeze that mocking smile upon their faces that accompanied this message.

PHYLO: (*Terrified*) For the gods' sake, whisper lest they should hear.

NOSOS: Let them hear it. Hear ye, gods! There is a Spartan still in existence who will fight against you if necessary, but will never endure such infamy!

PATON: Nosos, Nosos, think of victory. If they want to jest with us, then let them. They jest even amongst themselves.

EUPATOR: For the sake of victory, we must first triumph over ourselves.

PHYLO: Commander Nosos, we also have Sparta's interest at heart. So let us find the formula together, my commander, because you will continue to be a commander.

NOSOS: Well all right. Let the gods forgive me for the way I spoke. Have you got a candidate?

PHYLO: This is hard. It's very hard.

TINOS: There's no one like the prophecy calls for in Sparta.

PATON: But is it absolutely necessary that he be a Spartan?

EUPATOR: The prophecy doesn't specify that.

PHYLO: Perhaps we could choose a priest for a commander. Priests have good relationships with the gods.

NOSOS: Why not choose a wounded man ...

PATON: We have so many wounded that we could make a whole army out of them. But none of them are made for commanding.

TINOS: Say it, Eupator, speak up!

NOSOS: (*Suddenly realizing*) So you do have a candidate.

PHYLO: (*Rolling his eyes*) How could we have one when we haven't talked it over with you yet.

NOSOS: (*Bitterly*) And do you talk everything over with me first?

PHYLO: Of course we do. You are still the commander. And you will continue to be one of the commanders even after.

NOSOS: Speak up. Who's your candidate?

PATON: (*Hedging*) What does it matter who he is. The main thing is that the prophecy should fit him.

TINOS: The wish of the gods must be respected.

PHYLO: It's like one of those mathematical equations. Once the unknown is found, the solution presents itself.

EUPATOR: Speak simply, Phylo.

NOSOS: (*With growing rage*) Tell me his name!

PHYLO: His name. Someone else's name. What's in a name. Isn't one name much like another?

TINOS: Leave this to us, Nosos. We too are good patriots.

PHYLO: We are also Spartans.

PATON: Good Spartans.

NOSOS: (*As above*) I want to hear his name!

PHYLO: Then say it, ephor Eupator.

TINOS: Why wouldn't you say it?

PATON: Anyway, sooner or later everyone will know it.

EUPATOR: I could say it right now. Although there are a few other things we need to discuss.

NOSOS: (*Almost throwing a tantrum*) Nothing's more important.

PHYLO: That's true.

PATON: So let's have it, ephor Eupator. We too are curious.

TINOS: We're curious, though I'm consenting to it even beforehand.

NOSOS: (*Explodes*) For the gods' sake or the gods damn it—I want to hear his name!

EUPATOR: Tyrtaeus.

NOSOS: (*Relieved, he sighs*) I don't know him.

PHYLO: Didn't I tell you. It's only a name. It doesn't matter whose name.

NOSOS: Is he a Spartan?

PATON: Does it really matter where he's from. If he is good enough to be our commander, he'll be good enough to be a Spartan.

NOSOS: Does he live in Sparta?

PHYLO: Yes, he lives here amongst us and he knows our customs well.

NOSOS: Is he a guest or a slave?

PATON: A slave.

EUPATOR: He is a lame slave. From Messene.

NOSOS: Is he the one who was recently brought to Sparta as a captive?

EUPATOR: Do you know him?

NOSOS: (*With great dignity*) I know him, but I will never acknowledge him as the commander.

PHYLO: Think about the gods, I beg you. The message fits him perfectly. He is lame and yet he has a good mind.

NOSOS: (*He laughs in utter despair*) You've played a good jest on me, ephors. I swear, it would even appeal to the gods.

PATON: It's not a jest, Nosos. We asked him to be our commander, and he has accepted the post.

PHYLO: The smoke of his sacrifice has already drifted upwards.

EUPATOR: An unmistakable affirmation of his divine calling.

NOSOS: This is too fiendish even for a jest. To commit such foolishness with sober minds.

PATON: With sober minds, you say? But our belief in the gods exceeds soberness. And their wish cannot be foolish. If they want it, even a fool can do clever things. And clever things are not foolish. Surely, even you can't argue with that.

NOSOS: Well, then let the gods perish before Sparta is made to perish. Let the lot of them be impaled upon the sword if they demand conditions that cannot be undertaken with ancient honor.

EUPATOR: I object to your blasphemous words. Let such talk be reckoned as your own sin and not the sin of the people you sprang from.

NOSOS: The people I sprang from are noble. And they don't even want to live at such a price.

TINOS: The people don't want you, and they believe in the gods.

NOSOS: Well, I won't be in your way. I throw my commander's rank at your feet, ephor Eupator, like Phygon threw himself before us. Kick me as hard as you kicked Sparta, when you installed a Messene slave as its commander.

PATON: We did it for victory.

TINOS: For victory at all cost.

NOSOS: Even at the cost of Sparta!

PHYLO: What do you mean?

NOSOS: I mean that you struck at our very core. For the sake of the gods, you've chosen a commander who is a worse calamity for Sparta than a Messenean victory would be. Because Messene's defeat of Sparta would only be external, whereas the victory you're hoping for is anything but Spartan. With the concessions you've made to the gods, you've sacrificed the very essence of ancient Sparta. You did it believing that the affairs and decisions of the gods are so superior that they must be heeded over and above any national interest. This first time you are doing it for the sake of victory. Next time you'll do it voluntarily. Later still, you'll do it out of conviction and, finally, you'll do subserviently—melting into a community that no longer considers it crucial whether this one is Messenean or that one is Spartan. I see this as a giant trap, and I choose death rather than victory. Death here and now, the Spartan way, because victory at this price will be the first lost battle of an ultimate defeat. The years will accomplish the rest. And if you have a few more victories at such an exorbitant price, you'll be the ones who ransomed the essence of the Sparta for which you fought. And your fighting will become more and more immoral. Because you'll be fighting without knowing why— without a goal. And the things you would've preserved in the bitter brew of defeat will be lost in sacrificial victories. Ephors, you can still reverse all this. The fate of Sparta is now in your hands. Regardless of what the gods want, there is still a way out. But if you go through with what they want, you may be god-fearing men, but you'll be nothing other than traitors to your people.

EUPATOR: This is insane talk against the gods.

NOSOS: It is an insane act in the name of the gods.

SCENE 3

The scene is the same as in Act I, Scene 1, but the straw dummy is gone. Downstage right below the boulder, two women are cooking in two large cauldrons that are heated on open fires. Even if not fully visible, there are obviously many more cauldrons around—a big cook-up is in progress. The two women are bossed by the old midwife Amina. Quite a few spears are leaning against the base of the boulder.

1st WOMAN: I'm telling you, the lame one would come to grief if he goes out to the troops. They'll make a laughing stock of him. Has anyone ever heard the likes of it. A lame slave giving orders to Spartan troops.

2nd WOMAN: And a slave from Messene to boot.

AMINA: Just you go about your business. The lame one was sent by the gods. The word came from Delphi itself. To have him as our commander.

1st WOMAN: (*Flinging the answer over her shoulder*) He didn't hesitate to command us, women. Ordering us to cook up a hundred cauldrons of soup. Each big enough to fill the bellies of fifteen men.

2nd WOMAN: But there aren't even a hundred men in Sparta. All the able-bodied ones are out there, in battle. We only have the aged, the maimed and the children. So who are we cooking this enormous feast for?

1st WOMAN: For the Messeneans, I bet you.

AMINA: You stupid girl—their numbers are even more than a thousand times fifteen.

1st WOMAN: Tsk, tsk. You don't have to scoff so; just because you're ancient.

AMINA: Of course, you'd love it if the men came. At least a whole army.

1st WOMAN: I wouldn't even mind that. Because that's the worst in war. That the men are not at home. One can get used to hunger, even to seeing the dead. Just that one thing one can't get used to. I miss it a lot. Sometimes I even think of my own grand-father as a man.

2nd WOMAN: Just don't get a baby from him. Because you'd be giving birth to a bearded one.

AMINA: Keep that fire going.

1st WOMAN: Here comes Demetrios. How are you, fighter?

DEMETRIOS: (*A little out of breath*) Not yet, but I will soon be one.

1st WOMAN: You're already built like a man. And in other ways? (*The two women laugh together*)

AMINA: Control yourselves, you trollops.

DEMETRIOS: (*Embarrassed*) I am looking for the commander.

1st WOMAN: Perhaps he's with the army, your commander. That's where commanders are usually found.

AMINA: Don't pay any attention to them. They're rabid bitches, that's what they are. They taunt a man until he rapes them. And when he does, they rile him for having done it only once. Your commander hasn't been here, Demetrios. He's in a meeting with the ephors. But he'll be here soon.

DEMETRIOS: Then I'll wait for him here, Amina. I have impor-tant things to report to him.

1st WOMAN: And what would they be, laddie?

DEMETRIOS: I wouldn't tell it to you. Military secrets. So don't be curious.

AMINA: Just you keep on chopping the roots.

1st WOMAN: Why do you nag me? When one's husband has been a combat soldier for two years, she should love soldiers.

AMINA: Only your mouth is fouler than your blood. Hold your tongue; they're coming. (*Tinos, Eupator and Tyrtaeus arrive. They are talking among themselves*)

TINOS: Still, you should've gone out to the troops.

EUPATOR: No, Tinos. Tyrtaeus made the right decision. Had he gone out to them—in their first fit of rage, they might have torn him apart or made him run. Because the day they found out, they were really furious; but by the second day, they just grumbled. On the third day, they would've liked to see him already, and on the fourth, they were getting anxious as to why their commander had left them to themselves. And now, one after the other, runners arrive with messages from the captains, saying that the troops want to see their commander.

TINOS: Well then, you should go to them now, Tyrtaeus.

TYRTAEUS: No. It's not I who'll be going. They will be coming here. (*He turns in the direction of Demetrios*) Are you waiting for me, Demetrios? What have you to tell me, son?

DEMETRIOS: Good luck, commander.

TINOS: (*Sarcastically*) Is that the new greeting?

TYRTAEUS: (*Not reacting to the sarcasm*) Luck instead of greetings, because only with luck will we get to greet one another again. Demetrios, I'm listening.

DEMETRIOS: (*With a touch of self-importance*) The women could overhear it, my Lord.

TYRTAEUS: Noble Amina, could I ask you to move a little way from here.

1st WOMAN: (*Mumbling*) Three men at long last, and I have to leave. (*The three women exit*)

TYRTAEUS: So, Demetrios, what's the progress on the dyke?

DEMETRIOS: Everything is as you planned it. We finished the dyke. Five hundred boys worked on it for four days and nights. It already caused the water to swell enough to flood the valley. Except for the ridge on the hill, there's no other road between the cliff and the valley. And that ridge is barely a hundred thumbs wide.

TYRTAEUS: Good work, Demetrios. Tell them, I said so. Go now and don't forget about getting the bonfires ready at the gates of Sparta.

DEMETRIOS: That too shall be done, my Lord. (*He leaves*)

EUPATOR: Your plans are turning into reality, commander.

TYRTAEUS: It's strange to hear that word from your mouth.

EUPATOR: Yet you are that. Truly, the commander and I have come to believe it wholeheartedly.

TINOS: May the gods grant it so. Though I myself tend to believe in the kind of commander who rushes into battle at the head of his army, rather than one who weaves the plans in the background.

TYRTAEUS: We'll see. After so many lost battles, we'll win this one, and with it the war.

EUPATOR: You see, for me that's what's strange. To hear that we'll win. Coming from your mouth it sounds so natural. And yet it's not.

TYRTAEUS: One day you'll realize that it was.

TINOS: I understand it all, my commander, except for who will be the troops who will accomplish your wonderful plans, if not the ones who have fought for us this far.

TYRTAEUS: They will be different.

TINOS: Different, different but who?

TYRTAEUS: Let it be enough for you that they won't be the same. (*Amina comes running as much as she's able. The two other women follow after her a little later*)

AMINA: My Lord, the soldiers are grumbling and mutinous. They are coming this way fully armed. You must flee, because they're all saying that you are not their commander. They're making threats.

TYRTAEUS: (*With a strange cockiness*) Is that what they are doing? Of all the things Spartan fighters will resort to instead of winning battles. (*Noises of the approaching troops are heard*)

1st WOMAN: They're almost here. Look how skinny they are. They'd be a heavy burden rather than a sweet one. (*Pharon arrives with ten to fifteen soldiers. One of them in the forefront is Marcona*)

PHARON: Well, we've finally caught up with the lame one. You've been hiding yourself well for a commander.

TYRTAEUS: Who told you that I'm the commander?

PHARON: Look at that, he's playing the fool. Well, the pipers blew the signal for a new commander, and the captains announced that it was you. And I just kept on telling my mates that if you're our commander, we're not fighting.

TYRTAEUS: Who told you to fight? Marcona, maybe you know, since you're clutching your weapon with such determination. Who told you to fight? Perhaps you can tell us some other things as well: For instance, how many battles have you fought in?

MARCONA: In twenty-four battles, to the bitter end.

TYRTAEUS: Oh, that's wonderful. And how many times did you win?

MARCONA: Three times. (*The women giggle*)

TYRTAEUS: Three times out of twenty-four. Admirable. (*To the women*) Hush, women, don't you laugh. Such a determined fighter must be taken seriously. Three times out of twenty-four ...

PHARON: No matter what you say, we're never going back.

TYRTAEUS: Who told you to go back? Do what you feel like. After all, you're not even soldiers.

PHARON: How dare you say that.

TYRTAEUS: Oh you mustn't take it as an insult, but what would you call someone who won't acknowledge his commander; who will not fight though the battle is raging; who leaves his army of his own accord and doesn't want to return to it.

A VOICE: Pharon, you said that you know him well and you'll let him have it.

TYRTAEUS: So that's where it comes from. You still haven't filled your belly, noble Pharon; that's why you don't have enough discipline. Why didn't you ask the new commander for food? It would've been much smarter.

PHARON: What I'm asking ...

TYRTAEUS: (*With icy dignity*) Don't ask me for anything. Either I'm your commander, in which case you'd better vanish from my sight if you don't want me to get your blood for leaving the front; or I'm not your commander, in which case we have nothing to say to each other. (*He leaves*)

A VOICE: It looks as if you don't know him so well, Pharon.

ANOTHER VOICE: I swear, there's dignity even in the way he is limping. He is the commander after all.

TINOS: Well—and what are you waiting for? Aren't you ashamed of appearing like this before the ephors of Sparta?

MARCONA: Honorable ephors, it's so hard to explain. We've been misled.

EUPATOR: Begone, you violators of oaths—vanish. But before you go, take with you the orders as laid down by Tyrtaeus, your commander. Tell your captains and your lieutenants to guard the ridge on the hill, between the flood and the cliffs of Taygetos. Since the rest is flooded, we have no need of other soldiers. And even if we did, you wouldn't qualify. With the exception of the captains and the lieutenants, everyone's dismissed. Go wherever you please. From what I know about you, you will not be going forward anyway since the enemy is in that direction. About face! Move it! (*The soldiers with Pharon in the lead depart like beaten dogs*)

1st WOMAN: Phew, did the lame one do a good job on them or what?

2nd WOMAN: I feel sorry for them, their eyes nearly popped out at the sight of the soup. (*Tyrtaeus returns*)

EUPATOR: This was the first victory.

TYRTAEUS: Not yet the decisive one. But your attack from the flanks came at the right time, ephors. We pushed them into retreat, but how will we get them to march forward?

TINOS: I'm starting to believe that you can make miracles.

AMINA: (*Raptly*) Commander, we'll soon be finished with the soup. What should the women do?

TYRTAEUS: Supervise them, good Amina. Remember that the smell from each cauldron must hold fifteen fighters captive. Put the ringleaders, especially Pharon, to this one. It looks so good. (*He points to one of the cauldrons*) Be kind to them. Make them feel the warmth of home.

1st WOMAN: You don't have to tell us how to do that.

TYRTAEUS: Why not. That's your affair. But when the moon comes up, all the soldiers should be right here and well fed. Then when you hear the signal from the pipes and see the fires blazing, all of you must assemble here.

1st WOMAN: We will do it, commander, though I'd gladly fill the time of the full moon with fifteen men. (*Grinning, Tyrtaeus turns towards Eupator and Tinos. Photina comes with a basket on her arm*)

AMINA: (*Softly to Photina*) Photina, my precious, you got here. Well done. You brought the cheese, figs and the bread? (*Photina nods*) How clever of you. The meat is cooking. It'll be a good feed. (*Photina's basket of food stays on the ground*)

TYRTAEUS: Tinos, ephor, you are to be at the ridge on the hill.

And you, ephor Eupator, let half of the slaves go free. Let them see the demoralized Spartan troops retreating. Let them spread the news. Let the Messeneans rejoice and let their joy be premature.

EUPATOR: Good luck, commander.

TINOS: We will do as you commanded. (*Tinos and Eupator depart*)

PHOTINA: (*Slowly approaching Tyrtaeus, who's been standing with his back to her*) Tyrtaeus, commander ...

TYRTAEUS: (*Surprised, turns around*) Photina, the sweet Photina.

PHOTINA: (*Kindly*) I've heard from the heralds that you're the new commander. And I could see from your leg that you are Tyrtaeus. Otherwise I wouldn't have recognized you, because I always thought of you as one who lives in the clouds.

TYRTAEUS: "Dying and decision making can only be done in person." Isn't that what you said. Well I've made a decision—at worst, I'll die.

PHOTINA: But you've chosen Sparta.

TYRTAEUS: A new Sparta, whose laws will be different. Where life will be a joy.

PHOTINA: I told you once that you'll err with the decisive step. The Laws of Sparta are everlasting for Sparta. Whoever saves Sparta, saves its laws as well. The rattlesnake only gives up his rattles at the cost of his life.

TYRTAEUS: You must believe in a new Sparta, Photina. If it can have a lame commander, it's no longer the old Sparta.

PHOTINA: Only the prophecy made that possible. Otherwise they would never have consented to it. The prophecy and the utter despair that made them want to rid themselves of the responsibility. And you've accepted it from them voluntarily ...

TYRTAEUS: I could not have done otherwise. I am lame. And just this once, life made it possible for me to realize my dreams of becoming a hero in Sparta.

PHOTINA: Your real dreams were very different. Justice. Freedom. Peace.

TYRTAEUS: Those were my dreams. But now I'm halfway—on the border of dreams and reality. Can't you see that the olive trees of Sparta are waving back to me? The grave robber abandons his intent and utters a prayer. You don't understand this one, Photina. Go, cook soup.

PHOTINA: And perhaps even by tonight, I'll give birth to my child. (*She turns away from him. Demetrios arrives*)

DEMETRIOS: My commander, the bonfires are in readiness. At the sound of the first signal, we'll light them, and it will look as if the whole of Sparta is burning.

TYRTAEUS: Let the rest of the slaves go, so they can spread the news that we are setting fire to Sparta rather then allowing it get into Messenean hands. Then go, Demetrios, and chase all the women, the elderly and the children over here and place sentries at the gates so that no one can return to Sparta. And when you have lit the flames, come back here all of you.

DEMETRIOS: It shall be done, my commander. (*He departs*)

AMINA: (*Who's been listening*) Son, you've taken on an enormous task.

TYRTAEUS: (*To himself*) Will she still want to be mother to me when it's over.

2nd WOMAN: The lame one scares me so. He has such fervor. (*The first woman grins*) What is so amusing?

1st WOMAN: How strange his lovemaking must be.

PHOTINA: The birth pains are upon me. Amina!

AMINA: We've all felt them my girl.

PHOTINA: Help me, Amina, this is terrible.

AMINA: Look after things, you hussies, while I take her to a gentler, quieter place. (*Amina supports Photina, and they leave*)

1st WOMAN: (*Yelling after Amina*) But be sure to hurry back. The soups are almost ready.

2nd WOMAN: Look at that, they've come back. (*Marcona comes back with Pharon and the soldiers*)

MARCONA: We thought it over and came back.

1st WOMAN: You didn't have to be told twice to leave the front. To hell with all of you. Move over to the other cauldron. This one is for the leaders. Pharon, you can stay here. You too, Marcona. Since you are leaders—rebel leaders.

PHARON: Talk, useless words when nothing matters for us any more. Is your soup ready?

1st WOMAN: It's nearly there, chief. It'll be a good dish, though I can see on your face that it'll end up tasting bitter for you.

PHARON: (*Tastes it*) Damn it, it's too hot.

1st WOMAN: Come Marcona. Let's gather some wood. We'll need more for the fire. Leave your armor behind. You're heavy enough without it.

2nd WOMAN: (*To Pharon*) And you, don't you want to gather firewood ...

PHARON: (*Rudely*) I want to stuff my face.

2nd WOMAN: All right, all right, we're getting there. Amina will come back and add some salt to it. Then you can eat.

PHARON: I can eat it without salt so long as it's warm. Isn't that so, men, it just needs to be warm. I crave nothing as much as a bowl of hot soup.

1st SOLDIER: When was the last time we had a cooked meal?

2nd SOLDIER: I don't even know. My mother made me one a while back. She died since then.

PHARON: What are you preaching about? Since then, thousands have died, and now their faces are stuffed with sand. (*Amina returns*)

PHARON: Come, Amina, dish it out already.

AMINA: Not before the Commander comes back. (*Tyrtaeus returns*)

TYRTAEUS: Give it to them. It is not as if they're real soldiers who can wait for orders. (*Pharon, enraged, kicks over the cauldron*)

PHARON: Damn it, I've had enough of this kind of talk.

1st SOLDIER: (*Horrified*) All this precious soup and meat. Don't let it go to waste. (*With the exception of Pharon, all of them fall on their stomachs and gobble up the food from the ground*)

TYRTAEUS: (*Looks Pharon in the eye. After a little pause he bends down, takes a piece of cheese and some bread from the basket*) Remember, we've shared food together once.

PHARON: I don't want any. I'm up to my gullet with everything. (*He sits down*)

TYRTAEUS: Your helmet no longer sparkles, your shield is dirty, your spear is full of rust, and you haven't greased your moccasins for a long time. Don't be stubborn now, Pharon. Eat. Fill that emptiness, or your spine will snap. (*Pharon, shaking with agitation, stays silent*)

TYRTAEUS: Eat some cheese. You're so hungry. You could barely wait for the hot food to be ready. You must know that I cared for you from the first. You said yourself: lame one, with you one can't tell whether your outstretched arm will hit you on the head or support you under the arm. (*Pharon stays silent*)

TYRTAEUS: Don't you remember anything, Pharon? Not even the parade? A thousand divisions. A thousand times fifteen men. The crests of their helmets shining, shoulder taut against shoulder, and how the earth thundered. (*Pharon stays silent*)

TYRTAEUS: Don't you even remember what I told you: one has to hit you on the head first in order to be able to help you? Can't you understand that I'm only doing it to bring you out of your stupor?

PHARON: (*Talking towards the ground*) Give me some cheese.

TYRTAEUS: (*Sighing*) That's more like it. Here's some bread and olives. Figs too. Eat Pharon, otherwise all the bitterness will gobble you up.

PHARON: I'll fill my stomach one last time.

TYRTAEUS: Why do you talk like that when you won't ever go into battle again?

PHARON: But I won't survive the shame either. There's just one thing I'd like to know.

TYRTAEUS: What's that, Pharon?

PHARON: Why had I lived? And will anyone remember me?

TYRTAEUS: I would remember you, Pharon. If you could just understand that the decisive hour has come.

2nd WOMAN: The moon is out.

TYRTAEUS: And the hour is here. Will Sparta stand or fall? (*He climbs up on the cliff*)

VOICES: Flames have erupted from the direction of Sparta. Sparta is burning. (*Slowly the stage is engulfed in red*)

TYRTAEUS: (*Referring to the ashes of the fires that were under the cauldrons*) Oh, if only I could make those cinders rekindle under the ashes and have all of Messene burn. Will I have enough strength for that? (*Tinos and Eupator are hurrying back. They climb towards Tyrtaeus on the cliff*)

TINOS: May the gods grant it.

EUPATOR: All your plans are progressing smoothly so far. (*The sound of the flutes is heard—to assemble the people*)

TYRTAEUS: But how will it go from here? Thus far, I've only met with you, the leaders, who know much more about the issues than the people do. But now I'll have to talk to the people themselves. I'll need to stir up the kind of feelings they were never allowed to experience before. Feelings like a husband's compassion for his wife. A father's mercy for his newborn. The things that Sparta meant to them were lost, in the lost battles. And now their stifled instincts need to be aroused.

AMINA: The people are all coming this way. Terror and utter despair are written upon their faces.

EUPATOR: Tyrtaeus, you can't back away now. Your plans were their last hope. Just now do I truly understand the prophecy. It's with your words that you must light the greatest fire of all.

TYRTAEUS: These people have been fighting for so long that they've forgotten why they are fighting. And for centuries they've been taught that they're not allowed to do anything for themselves. That they exist only for the sake of serving Sparta. But by now everything that was Spartan has disappeared from their souls, leaving emptiness in its place. Yet the long wars have also acquainted them with the lives of other peoples. Perhaps now, they'd rather think of adopting the others' way of life than extinguish it.

TINOS: (*Standing next to Tyrtaeus on the cliff*) They're coming like a swirling deluge. Do what you can.

PHARON: Like livestock when they sense fire ... Then I'm going. I have nothing to do with them.

TYRTAEUS: You're not going anywhere, because you belong to where the flames are coming from. You stand here in the front line.

PHARON: That I won't do.

TYRTAEUS: You won't do it? All right, so don't do it. But if you go now, you will never find out why being alive would have been worthwhile. (*He turns to Tinos and asks, in a quiet voice*) Tinos, did you arrange what I had asked?

TINOS: The spy has been briefed. He'll report what you wanted him to report. The veterans you want to address are wearing little bunches of grass upon their helmets. Their scars have been touched up with paint.

TYRTAEUS: Amina, I hear that Photina is about to give birth. When will her child arrive?

AMINA: Possibly by morning.

TYRTAEUS: Then take another newborn in your arms, and if I ask you, say that it's a boy and that his mother just gave birth to him. Let us regard it as a sign from the gods.

AMINA: I'll do it for Sparta and for you.

TYRTAEUS: You put your trust in a Messenean slave?

AMINA: I put my trust in the commander of Sparta.

TYRTAEUS: (*Turns away from all those who are present*) And now help me, ye gods. Help me though I am two times a traitor. For I betrayed Messene, and I betrayed myself. I am about to commit a sin. Yet not committing it would also be a sin. I must arouse the people's emotions in any way I can. That's why I've never gone to the theater. So I wouldn't witness the inducement of true emotions through untrue words.

EUPATOR: You are asking a people to answer for themselves. Whether they'll live or die, let their conduct be worthy of Sparta. (*Voices from a crowd coming close*)

VOICES: Where's the lame one? Sparta is burning! Perish, the traitor! Where is that Messenean slave? Our children are burning in the fire. My father, oh my poor, helpless, blind old father. (*The crowd pours onto the stage. Of the three veterans who wear bunches of grass on their helmets, the first one has terrible touched-up scars on his chest; the second has one forearm missing and the third is blind*)

TYRTAEUS: (*At first he looks at them almost helplessly, then slowly he toughens and bursts out*) Back off, you worthless cowardly people who are escaping like a herd of cattle— back off. Don't let your ugly talk rise up to the commander who was appointed by the gods. Because by Zeus, I'll throw his bolts of lightning upon your heads. You are lamenting about Sparta, you filthy bunch, yet no viler sons of man had ever left it in the lurch. Yes it's true, I, a Messenean slave, have to raise my voice; I, who was bewitched by the many virtues of Sparta, which are no longer in evidence amongst you and came to my ears only from the mouth of bards. You filthy, spineless lot; you wouldn't mind retreating further and further, far away from Sparta, giving up all that is Spartan, abandoning the graves of the ancients, becoming slaves in foreign lands. But I, the commander, will not allow it. I've drawn a wall of fire behind you, cowards. Perish here, contemptible ones, be one with the mire of this land, but don't let your moccasins carry the sacred dust of this fatherland into faraway slavery. I won't let an army of running Spartans bring dishonor upon the name of the invincible Hercules, from whose blood you have sprung. Oh gods, oh gods, how awful that the commander must put a wall of flame behind his troops to stop them from retreating. Is this why you trained through countless hours of physical exercise, so you can run away from the enemy? Oh gods, why couldn't I be the kind of commander who can send his troops into battle with true and noble words: Forward courageously, the gods have never yet abandoned thee! You're wailing about your blind father, good sons that you are, who'd leave him here for the slave chain, because Sparta doesn't even mean as much to you as saving your stricken old father. Where are the times when you were taught to be ashamed if you hadn't put Sparta even before the gods themselves. Let no one fear, let no one dread, however many be our enemy because it's not death but shame that you, Spartans, must now fear the most. Behind you is a wall of flame that guarantees that you'll never be slaves, because the enemy will throw you upon their swords if you do not rush forward and charge into their front line.

A VOICE: Enough of fighting, we want peace.

TYRTAEUS: Hah, let everyone spurn life as they spurn the enemy, if peace means only shame and slavery. The time for making peace is over, and whoever throws away their sword will be killed with the same sword by morning. His wife will be defiled by multiple rape, his infant will be beaten to death and the last seed of the Spartan race will be lost by tomorrow. So be merciful and kill them here and now. Let death appear to them in the beautiful shades of the reddening dawn. Kill them with the same weapons that you no longer dare to use against the enemy. Kill the women so they don't have to endure defilement upon their bodies. Kill the children so they cannot be taken away as slaves. Massacre your own kind if you cannot defend the race. I command you to lift up your swords, and you, mothers, be compliant and happy that you will not be made pregnant by the drunken troops of the enemy. (*A frozen silence lasting for a few seconds ...*) Not a single woman or child cried out against my command. That is proof of how the future is judged by the worthier half of the population. Death rather than dishonor. From now on, you, women and children, will be my army and we shall die without a single cry of anguish for a Sparta in which all the ancient virtues have died out in the men.

AMINA: My commander, we shall be your army.

TYRTAEUS: The whole world will be astonished by this combat. Women and children will go into battle and the men will cook the soup. Mothers will use their babies as shields on their arms, while the men will be throwing chicken bones at each other. And while the mothers suckle their babes on blood instead of milk, the men will crawl under the goats, suck milk from their teats and make love to each other.

1st VETERAN: We elders have never known such dishonor.

TYRTAEUS: Step forward, noble fighter, and tell us where you received that terrible scar on your chest.

1st VETERAN: At Panthos, where the enemy was ten times as many as we were, yet singing Spartan songs and bleeding from a hundred wounds, we were still victorious.

TYRTAEUS: Oh, Panthos, what feelings your name must arouse

in the hearts of true warriors. And you, old fighter, where did you lose half of your arm?

2nd VETERAN: (*Whose lower right arm is missing*) At Samos. But before I lost it, that half arm of mine caused the loss of twenty Messeneans.

TYRTAEUS: Samos, where the Spartan troops were surrounded—and yet we've won, because Spartan beliefs still lived in the hearts of our fighting men. And you, old friend, I see that you're blind.

3rd VETERAN: And still I have seen more in my life, and more of what's praiseworthy than you have, commander. I've seen a thousand and six hundred of the enemy killed at Phykos. And they had five times as many wounded.

TYRTAEUS: What those times must have been like! Always against ten times as many, and always bordering on a miracle from the gods. (*The spy pushes his way through the crowd with feverish excitement*)

SPY: Make way, let me pass. I have important news for the commander.

TYRTAEUS: So speak! Briefly and clearly.

SPY: My Lord, the Messenean army is transported with joy. At first, when our soldiers retreated from the battlefield, they were suspicious of being tricked. But when the freed Messenean slaves told them how terrified our troops were, and when they saw that Sparta was burning, the flames of their joy reached even higher than our wall of fire. They made a victory feast, and now every one of them is lying in a drunken stupor in their tents.

TYRTAEUS: Oh, what an opportunity this would be for a surprise attack.

A VOICE: It's true. By the gods it is true.

TYRTAEUS: (*To the spy*) You're discharged. And what do you hold in your arms, good Amina?

AMINA: A newly born. A newborn son. Has there ever been a more auspicious sign?!

TYRTAEUS: (*Theatrically gets down on his knees*) The gods have granted us a sign of their favor: It would border on the miraculous because the troops of our enemy are ten times as many, but we could now be victorious.

1st VETERAN: Then lead us into battle.

TYRTAEUS: There isn't anyone I could lead into battle, my good warrior. With old men, women and children, I couldn't defeat even a drunken army. (*He kicks a stone with his foot. The stone rolls down and topples the bunch of spears that are leaning against the base of the boulder*) Look at that—even the spears appear to want to fight, but there's no one to pick them up and throw them at the enemy.

PHARON: (*Bends down and picks up a spear*) By Hercules, I'll take one.

THE CROWD: Me too, me too. Let's go against Messene. Let us avenge the disgrace. (*They are fighting for the spears*)

TYRTAEUS: Stop. Kill the enemy not each other.

2nd VETERAN: By the gods, he speaks well. He truly is our commander.

TYRTAEUS: Oh, Spartans, if you will fight the enemy as you fought for spears, our victory will be as certain as the rising of the sun. But wait for just a blink of an eye. You too, Pharon, because a task awaits you. We'll ambush the enemy on the ridge between the flood and the rock face. Advance quietly until you hear the signal from the pipes. They must be taken completely by surprise. Let every warrior wrap a white rag on his left arm. That's how we'll recognize each other in the darkness. And you, women and children, must help us terrify the enemy by yelling and screaming wildly. Go now, and may luck be with you. Our slogan is: victory or death. (*The crowd leaves quietly*) Ephors, and you, noble Pharon, listen to me. You are to take over the command. Ephor Tinos, you will command the left flank. Your troops are to push them into the water. The right flank is to be commanded by ephor Eupator, whose army will chase the enemy onto the cliffs. Pharon will command the reserves.

PHARON: Grant me a request concerning the great honor that you bestowed upon me. Allow me to be the one who commands the right flank. Ephor Eupator is more advanced in age. Let him stay with the reserves.

EUPATOR: Let it be as he wishes. All of a sudden it's very important to him.

PHARON: After so many disappointments, that's hardly surprising.

TYRTAEUS: Your wish is granted. You are to command the right flank.

PHARON: (*To Tyrtaeus*) Everything will be done as you have commanded, and we will be victorious.

TINOS: May the gods and the spirit of the ancients be with us. (*They are about to leave when Pharon stops himself*)

PHARON: I am going to my troops now. Tyrtaeus, you will remember me, won't you, if I don't come back? You promised.

TYRTAEUS: May the gods be with you, commander Pharon. I will never forget you. (*Pharon leaves. There's silence. Only Amina and two heralds stay on the stage with Tyrtaeus. The heralds will soon sound the signal with modern day trumpets that are not yet visible*)

A deadly silence has fallen on the terrain. The battlefield is as silent before the combat as the cemetery is after it. The struggle I'm now leading is the kind I have always struggled against. And the victory I'll reap will be the cause of my destruction.

AMINA: I know, because I know your secret. The only struggle greater than the one about to be fought on the battlefield is the one that must now be ravaging your soul.

TYRTAEUS: You know my secret, Amina, for I don't have any other secret than my lameness.

AMINA: And that you were allowed to grow up with it. Blood cannot be turned into water.

TYRTAEUS: Blood will turn into more blood and pour from the heads and hearts of the fighting men. Blood will congeal in the veins of those who have grown cold. Blood will turn into more blood, not into water. I wish it had turned into water, so that I could've drowned in my own veins.

A RUNNER: (*Hurries in*) Commander, the troops are ready for battle.

TYRTAEUS: Sound the signal! (*The trumpets are blown. The sound*

Tyrtaeus: A Tragedy

of the Marseillaise is heard, followed by tumultuous battle cries, becoming a little more subdued as Tyrtaeus, to the accompaniment of the music, begins to recite)

You who have sprung from the blood of the invincible Hercules,
Forward courageously, the gods have never yet abandoned thee.

Let no one fear, let no one dread, however many be our enemy,
Forward, shields in hand, charge into their front lines.

Hah, let every one spurn life as they spurn the enemy,
Let death appear to them in the beautiful shades of the
                                        [reddening dawn.

Those who live with a heroic heart, compact into a valiant band,
And at the pinnacle man fights against man in sight of the
                                        [warriors.

And if they die, their death is different, for they were their
                                        [people's sentinels,
But the ones who tremble, the ones who dread, will be cursed by
                                        [eternal infamy.*

* Translator's note: Lajos Walder has the fictional Tyrtaeus recite the historical Tyrtaeus' second surviving battle hymn in Antal Radó's Hungarian translation, which my English version is based on. Incidentally, Radó's version greatly differs from the standard English version of the hymn by J. Banks and J. M. Chapman (London, 1876).

ACT III

Eupator's tent. The Ephors are conferring. Nosos is not among them.
Tyrtaeus is the fifth Ephor. A soldier is guarding the entrance.

TYRTAEUS: And how did Pharon die?
EUPATOR: He charged ahead as if possessed. He cut such a path with his sword that no one could match him. He fought like that for perhaps as much as half of an hour, when suddenly he came face to face with a Messenean who was yelling furiously: "Where's Tyrtaeus, the traitor—two times the traitor! First, for wanting to betray his fatherland, and second, for betraying the homeland that raised him." Pharon roared back at him with all his might, "Do not foulmouth my commander, because I'll smash your face to bits," and with a single slash of his sword, he cut the Messenean in half. But this left him defenseless for a moment, and that's when he was stabbed with a deadly javelin.
TYRTAEUS: Who was the Messenean?
EUPATOR: Some weaver of sorts. A weaver of hemp. He commanded one of the battalions. Dainos was his name. The shock caused by his death contributed to their downfall.
TYRTAEUS: (*Dully*) I knew him. I knew him so well. He was my father in place of my father—he raised me. (*Short pause*) What happened to Teknon?
TINOS: Before the moon came up and the fires were lit, Lukianos raped him, and in his shame, Teknon drowned himself.
PHYLO: The gods punished Nosos because he blasphemed against them and went against their wishes.
EUPATOR: When the gods want to destroy someone, first they take away his mind.
PHYLO: And that's what happened to him. When you, honored Tyrtaeus, gave the command to feign a retreat, he suspected treachery and cursed "that lame Messenean slave." In his rage, he charged against the enemy like a demented bull, he alone

against the thousands. He didn't even get past the advance guard before he was hacked to pieces.

TINOS: I was against him, ephors, but now I feel deeply moved. Truly, he only had one sin, a sin that is perhaps even more beautiful than any virtue. He loved his country above all ...

TYRTAEUS: Photina ...?

EUPATOR: Gave birth to a hunchback son. According to our laws, as laid down by Lycurgus, her baby will be abandoned on the cliffs of Taygetos.

TYRTAEUS: How awful are these deaths and all the wretchedness for the sake of a single victory.

PHYLO: Oh yes, victory comes at a high price!

TYRTAEUS: No one has paid the price I'm paying for it.

PATON: This is your day, Tyrtaeus. Do not bother yourself with little things. You are a victorious commander, and we have chosen you as an ephor in place of Nosos.

TYRTAEUS: The high rank which fell to me from Nosos, who died in battle, is a most honorable one, but I can hardly honor myself now ...Those little things dwarf the bigger ones for me ... I wish I hadn't done it ... I wish I hadn't done it ... The spell of this soil triumphed over me, triumphed in place of me, and yet I feel that I've lost. Because I was victorious only once, but I have so many, many losses ...

TINOS: These are words, merely words. A battle must have its dead.

EUPATOR: Even ordinary life has its dead. But Sparta must live. (*Noise from outside*)

GUARD AT THE DOOR: (*Blocks the entrance with his spear and then announces*) Noble ephors, Photina is here. She asks to be allowed in. She wants to be heard.

EUPATOR: No woman can ever enter here.

TYRTAEUS: Let her in. It is my wish.

PHYLO: (*Hiding his feelings to the contrary*) You are still the commander... (*Photina is allowed in. She carries her baby in her arms*)

PHOTINA: It is with your permission that I'm here Tyrtaeus, though there is no power on earth that could have held me back.

PHYLO: Your manner of speaking does not take into account who we are.

PHOTINA: Oh, I'm far from wanting to bring your anger upon my head. I came for your compassion; that you be merciful with my tiny son. Hear me.

PHYLO: That's more respectful. I propose that we hear her out.

TYRTAEUS: Will you be quiet already ...

PHYLO: I find the manner in which you talk to me strange, to say the least, noble commander. Because you still are the commander. Though there's much you can thank me for.

TYRTAEUS: The things I can thank you for, merit no thanks.

EUPATOR: Why have you come here, Photina, when you know that women are never allowed in here?

PHOTINA: ... I know it well. But I've become a mother.

PATON: The law ...

PHOTINA: ... doesn't allow it. But can there be a law that's stronger than the law of nature? Even the female wolf will not let her pup be torn away from her teats.

TYRTAEUS: Speak differently, Photina. As befits a woman. Gently, like the sound of the Euboean flute...

PHOTINA: I cannot be gentle now. I am like iron softened by the sledgehammer until it becomes diamond hard. (*Almost crying*) Look at the eyes of this tiny child. Look at his eyes and nothing else. See how they sparkle with intelligence. His father and mother are both good Spartans. A Spartan woman cut his umbilical cord, and the knife she used was a well serving Spartan sword.

PHYLO: But he's a hunchback.

PHOTINA: If a commander can be lame in Sparta, then a child can be a hunchback. Because of a tiny hump you want to abandon him on the cliffs of Taygetos.

TINOS: Order demands it so.

PHOTINA: Oh, you still dare to talk about order. What order? Whose order? The order of nature or chaos? For nine months I carried this darling little boy and I craved for him so much that had I craved for a pearl as much, my womb would've given birth even to a pearl. Yet even on a pearl there is some irregularity, a tiny flaw that is a part of it. But who would think of throwing it back into the ocean because of that....

EUPATOR: Who taught you to speak thus? Words like that from the mouth of a Spartan woman ...

PHOTINA: The truth taught me ...

PHYLO: The law is the truth.

PHOTINA: Provided that the law is just. I know very well what the law prescribes: Let the child be faultless like cattle, shaped to perfection like the slender spear. The Spartan millet is so scarce that there isn't enough for a cripple.

PHYLO: You are a clever daughter of Sparta.

PHOTINA: Help me now, or else Sparta will become my wicked stepmother forever. I was always the first in running; no one bore hunger better than me. I boxed so well that more than one man's nose cracked under the weight of my punches. I trained and endured through dark nights, chilly dawns and hot afternoons, just so I'd become faultless, and have the seed faultless within me; the seed that would one day ripen into a son. And now, a tiny hump between the shoulder blades of a little boy is the crucial refutation of your regime. And I put it to you, that the fault may well have been not within, but outside of me.

EUPATOR: Photina, think of what you're saying. Our laws were given to us by Lycurgus, who commanded us not to alter them until he returns. And whosoever attempts to change them, or dares to judge them ...

PHYLO: (*Threateningly towards Tyrtaeus*) ... provokes the law against himself ... (*Mellifluously*) ... My daughter, be clever, not reckless.

TYRTAEUS: But she is clever. And the fountain that's gushing out of her now is the kind that bores through layer upon layer, for years on end. And when it finally breaks through, it cannot be sealed as if it were of goatskin. Go on, Photina; We have won, so we have time for reflection.

TINOS: (*Scornfully*) Today is your day, Tyrtaeus, and you are fond of fanciful words.

PHOTINA: Ephors, living fathers of Sparta. You must find it awful to hear such rebellious words. But ever since I gave birth to my child—this child, whom the laws of Sparta want to annihilate because of a tiny hump, I am no longer a Spartan. Just a mother. The mother of a little boy who has a disability. The mother of a child who has a right to live. You talk about laws that were created by Lycurgus and that he forbade you to change. But who amongst you has ever seen Lycurgus, that you can justify believing every single word you attribute to him. The only rightful law is the one that naturally lives in every person. A law that is outside of human nature is no longer human and above all not humane. You're always deferring to Lycurgus, but he could have erred. He did err, if his laws stand outside of us. Two laws collide here before you: the law of humans, which belongs to nature and is therefore natural; and an external law that is outside of us and is therefore unnatural. You have the task of deciding which is the genuine one, bearing in mind that appearances can be many, but there can be only one truth.

PATON: Who taught you these words?

PHOTINA: The sleepless nights.

PHYLO: Who contaminated you like this?

PHOTINA: The doubts.

PHYLO: The people of Sparta do not doubt.

PHOTINA: You are so right, the constant physical exercise Lycurgus prescribed, leaves no time for thinking. And doubt can only come to those who think.

PATON: You are a woman, you have other tasks.

PHOTINA: My task is the same as that of a cow. To calf each year, preferably bulls.

TINOS: Women don't usually talk like that.

PHOTINA: And the men, how do the men talk in Sparta? They don't even have a word for making love. A few frenzied and violent movements serve in its place. In other lands, women cover their bodies with perfumed oils and silk to heighten their charms for their man. But we, the women of Sparta, are like bare, two-legged milking cows who only have value when pregnant. Should a caprice of fate render one of us barren, each night, shamefaced and stealthy like a thief, a different man may scurry into her tent to discharge upon her body the function common to all men. This too is a law of the great Lycurgus and that it should occur only in the dead of night, only in darkness. And any man may use her, since like a barren cow —a barren woman is worthless. You say that I speak as though I wasn't even a woman. Well, I heard of ships that come from countries where women have rights as if they were men. Of cities where women wear garlands made of flowers around their necks and precious jewels in their hair. Where they use paints to hide the wrinkles etched upon their faces—because I have never ever heard of a city or country where women do not suffer in place of men. As you can see, noble Lords, I stand before you in the coarsest garb. I have no silk, flower, oil or paint. There isn't any softness within me, and I know nothing about the games of love so sweetly told by a distant song. My body is covered with rough hardened skin, there's nothing within me that is gentle, nothing that's feminine. I am like a female animal that doesn't know and doesn't want to know the laws of Lycurgus, who understands only what nature instilled in her: the law of motherhood. I have no other beautiful jewel than the child I hold in my arms. He is the meaning of my life. On that very first night I desired to fall pregnant as eagerly as a child desires a sweet fruit, lest as a barren woman I should become every man's bitch; because I was hoping that one day, another kind of man may come along. One who doesn't just talk about what I cooked today; what his meal is going to be. Aside from my husband, who behaved strictly in accordance with the law, I hoped one day to belong to such a man. My baby can now protect me from becoming as communal as the meals are in Sparta. He makes it possible for me to have my own tent, and my own fireside, where I can reflect upon the monstrousness of the real freak who made life so harsh that instead of peace and prosperity, he turned reproduction and war into the goals of the state.

EUPATOR: My daughter, you can't know what you're saying. The hurt has taken away your mind, or perhaps it was the fever, which women sometimes get when giving birth. Go, Photina, now, leave the ephors' tent ... the law as decreed by Lycurgus will be enforced.

PHOTINA: Oh, forget that awful tyrant who perhaps didn't even have a groin, so stubborn and obstinate is the rage he spreads around himself. How much can women mean to him, who was childless and mateless. In vain he preaches about the glories of pregnancy and carries on about solstice celebrations for boys, when what he would really have liked is fighters giving birth to armed fighters. That's why he secretly prescribed that they should love each other. If they were able to conceive, perhaps then he could successfully control nature and avoid reproduction's slow, protracted course. Between women and men it happens only in the darkest night. And it doesn't matter with whose partner. The law consents to a pause only when conception had occurred. Only then does being in heat become useless. Oh, Tyrtaeus, how I detest the one who made such a cold and rigid regime out of joy.

TYRTAEUS: You're the one who's talking, Photina, not me ...

PHOTINA: But you've led me onto this path. Now I understand all that I couldn't grasp before, but which disturbed me. Behind a rigid regime there's nothing but chaos, and nature itself cries out for help. Why give birth to a child here when they will tear him from his mother's embrace even while he is little, so having been robbed of any feelings of family, he should sacrifice his life to the impotent and joyless Lycurgus. (*She starts to sob and the little baby starts to cry in her arm*)

PATON: Photina, be silent. Don't say another word. (*Tyrtaeus goes to Photina. He is looking at the little boy*)

PHYLO: (*Meanwhile whispering to Tinos*) The lame one is growing on top of us. It was he who spoke through Photina. This is his agenda. What will become of Sparta if we allow this?

TINOS: (*Responding in a whisper*) It's you who wanted him to be the leader.

PHYLO: I wanted him back then. Even he was good for it then.

We'd have made even a fat-bellied cat into our leader, had the prophecy said so.

TINOS: He defended Sparta.

PHYLO: And now we have to defend Sparta from him.

TINOS: You are plotting to destroy him. You're betraying him.

PHYLO: I am doing neither. I am merely being a real-politician.

TYRTAEUS: (*Gently towards Photina*) Is your little boy hungry? (*Slowly he is separating himself from the other ephors*) Feed him, Photina. (*He sits her down. She turns away and starts feeding the newborn*) What a sweet child. He resembles you, you know. (*Photina nods. Tyrtaeus turns toward the ephors*) Look at him, noble Lords. He already seems to have had enough. Perhaps he wasn't even hungry. Come noble Lords look at him. You know what, Photina, give him to me. I will take him to Sparta's famous ephors. Who knows if one day he might not become an ephor himself. (*Takes the baby from Photina to the ephors*) So let him get to know them. Tinos, my friend, I wonder if you can recall if there was ever a disabled athlete winning a competition in the stadium?

TINOS: I have to think a little. Yes, I do remember. The one-armed smith from Pindaros. He came first in discus throwing and gained fame for Pindaros. (*He goes to look at the baby*)

TYRTAEUS: So this little one can even be an athlete.

PHYLO: (*Fawning*) I also know of a famous orator who had a speech impediment and yet he became the best orator of his country.

TYRTAEUS: And Homer ...

EUPATOR: He was blind, it's true, yet he knew that the dawn is rose-fingered.

PATON: (*With complicity*) You're a clever man, Tyrtaeus. I've been observing how you cast your net over the ephors. But do you know, this little one does remind me of my grandchild. He has the very same eyes.

TYRTAEUS: Noble ephor, is it possible that you too have tasted the forbidden fruit? (*All the men laugh. Embarrassed, Photina turns away, and Tyrtaeus gives the child back to her*) Good ephors, how well laughter melts away the floodgates of the heart. If you don't look at things so rigidly perhaps you will also arrive at another point of view. In the beginning, Sparta was small. The laws it needed then were different from the laws it needs today. If Lycurgus hadn't given such strict laws to the ancients, laws that made it impossible for people to grow soft, perhaps Sparta would've perished long ago. But the world goes forward and Sparta, the grown man, cannot wear the moccasins of Sparta, the child, because they no longer fit.

TINOS: (*Who's leaning over the baby*) Look, how the little bugger squeezed my hand. (*Noise is heard from outside the tent*)

PATON: (*Looking toward the entrance*) What is it?

TYRTAEUS: Ephors, let's make a quick decision. Let us defend the little boy before the people.

TINOS: I'll stick up for him. Judging by the way he gripped my finger, he can still be a good discus thrower.

TYRTAEUS: And you, ephor Eupator ...? (*Leukos suddenly jumps in through the entrance. He takes two steps forward, and then he spreads his legs apart and puts his hands on his hips. The people throng after him right up to the entrance of the tent*)

LEUKOS: At last we caught up with the fugitives. Photina and her crippled infant are here. So this is where she fled from the decision of our council. (*Contemptuously*) It looks as though she came to the right place.

EUPATOR: Speak more respectfully, Leukos. You stand before the ephors, the leaders elected by the people.

LEUKOS: Don't waste your words. We're taking Photina's cripple to the cliffs of Taygetos. Or had you, ephors, decided otherwise?

PHYLO: I uphold the laws of Sparta.

LEUKOS: Then we needn't talk further.

EUPATOR: (*Sarcastically*) Particularly, since we, ephors, haven't yet made a decision!

LEUKOS: Have you heard that, Spartans? Ephor Eupator uttered those very words. Make sure you don't forget his name. The ephors had not yet made a decision. But can there be a decision contrary to what our laws tell us! Sparta has no need of imbeciles or cripples. Sparta needs only fighters. To the Taygetos with the freaks. (*Tyrtaeus is visibly shaken*)

TINOS: Leukos, tell us how many battles you fought in. Or was it laurels you brought us from the stadium?

LEUKOS: Look at that, Tinos as well. One wouldn't have thought that you, of all people, will stick up for cripples.

PATON: Everyone will think what he's capable of thinking.

LEUKOS: It's a conspiracy. You're all defending the beautiful Photina. But have you considered how many fathers a freak like that must have. (*He calls through the opening of the tent*) Largos come forward. (*Largos comes into the tent*)

LEUKOS: People of Sparta, pay attention. Sparta's honor is at stake. (*To Largos*) Identify yourself.

LARGOS: I am a Spartan fighter and citizen.

LEUKOS: Have you been in combat?

LARGOS: I fought in over fifteen battles.

LEUKOS: Your wife?

LARGOS: Photina ... over there.

LEUKOS: The one who bore you a cripple? (*Largos nods*) And are you familiar with the laws of Sparta?

LARGOS: I am.

LEUKOS: Were they not the laws of your father and your grandfather?

LARGOS: ... and of my grandfather's grandfather.

LEUKOS: Do you recognize that this law ... protects ...

LARGOS: ... Sparta and the Spartans.

LEUKOS: What does the law say?

LARGOS: It says that the millet and all produce are scarce in Sparta. So we can only accept the able-bodied newborns into our community.

LEUKOS: There is no doubt about it! You do know the law, soldier. The people of Sparta can be proud of the fact that over here even common soldiers know the law. At least, this way they will not be swayed by the whim of the leaders.

EUPATOR: Leukos, your conduct is tantamount to demagoguery. You want to rise through us.

LEUKOS: (*Doesn't pay any attention to him*) Largos, do you expect us to raise your crippled son on our meager crops.

LARGOS: No, I don't. Of course I don't. (*He falls out of the role-playing expected of him*) But ... (*He points to Photina*) ... She said that she'll throw herself off the cliff ... and I don't want that either.

LEUKOS: (*Hissing*) Pull yourself together, you fool. Ephors, surely we cannot add anything to this subject. My question is straightforward. Can we admit a crippled infant to the community of Spartans? (*Toward the crowd*) People of Sparta, is this or is this not the issue?

CROWD: It is Leukos.

LEUKOS: We'll start with ephor Eupator. Answer my question. Yes or no?

EUPATOR: No.

LEUKOS: Ephor Tinos?

TINOS: No.

LEUKOS: Phylo, I am sure you'll say no.

PHYLO: I'll say no.

LEUKOS: One need not even ask Paton. He knows the law so well.

PATON: Take care, Leukos, for I know it extremely well.

LEUKOS: Your vote?

PATON: No.

LEUKOS: Your vote is the last, Tyrtaeus. It's your turn.

TYRTAEUS: It was clever of you to make me last, Leukos. Had you asked me first, the outcome would've been different. But since you did have to ask me, you had better listen. And you, ephors and Spartans, listen to me, all of you. The question he put to us is like a double-edged dagger. If I grab hold of it to push it away from me, it will cut my hand; and if I don't push it away from me, in the hands of a clever demagogue it will stab me through the heart wherever I am. Spartans, the question is like that double-edged dagger; yet I know where my answer lies.

EUPATOR: Spartans, do not forget that we owe our victory and the survival of Sparta to Tyrtaeus alone.

TYRTAEUS: Ephor Eupator, though this praise came from you,

I cannot accept it, because I did not come here for Sparta's victory. I came to plot its destruction...

LEUKOS: Do you hear what he's saying?

TYRTAEUS: I came to plot your destruction, Sparta, though I, myself, am a Spartan. (*A murmur of surprise*)

EUPATOR: Speak, Tyrtaeus. Validate yourself. Thus far I was the only one who knew your secret; that's why I trusted you.

THE VOICE OF AMINA FROM THE CROWD: I too trusted you, because a Spartan sword cut your umbilical cord.

TYRTAEUS: There must be many among you who knew my dead father and mother. As Largos said, both of them had Spartan grandfathers whose grandfathers were also Spartans. My father died in battle, before I was born. My mother's labor pains lasted for two days. Her newborn son, had one leg shorter than the other. Knowing what the inhuman laws of Lycurgus meant, she did not hesitate for a moment. Feverish and bleeding, she tied me to herself and staggered towards Messene. Sparta had no need of me back then.

LEUKOS: You braggart.

TYRTAEUS: No, Leukos, I'm not bragging. I just want to point out to the citizens of Sparta that a person with a disability can also bring glory to his country. My mother set off towards Messene. Her strength left her on the journey, but she continued in a delirious state, so determined was she to get me to Messene. I often hoped that in her final moments she was no longer aware of the pain she endured. When she collapsed just past the border, Pardophoros, the shepherd found us. Before the beloved woman died, she told him the secret of my origins. Pardophoros shook his right fist towards Sparta and with his left hand closed my mother's eyes.

LEUKOS: His every word betrays gods and country.

TYRTAEUS: Is it the truth you want to hear, or one of those fairytales for children.

PATON: We want to hear the truth.

PHYLO: (*Hatefully*) Although one cannot be certain that he's telling the truth.

TYRTAEUS: Let those who listen to me decide whether I do or not. Pardophoros took me into Messene, to a worthy citizen, who had a reputation for being humane. He was young then, that weaver of hemp whom Pharon killed in the battle yesterday. And it was I who put the sword into the hands of Pharon. That's how I lost my father, my mother and my stepfather. All of them because of Sparta.

LEUKOS: With every word the lame one slanders you.

TYRTAEUS: I grew up in Messene, where famous philosophers taught me, but I must admit that neither boxing nor wrestling featured among my subjects. The content of those teachings is foreign to you, Spartans. We pondered what type of government is the best; what rights befit human beings; how to distinguish good from bad; what is real behind appearances; what are the pathways of the stars; how the hypotenuse relates to the perpendicular, and how best to construct a tympanum. In short, all those subjects about which here in Sparta a boy hears little and a girl even less. So Messene was a very different world, foreign to everything that's Spartan. And it's with those wholly different beliefs that I viewed the cruelties committed here in Sparta. I felt hatred towards Sparta as did all the Spartan exiles who lived in Messene. I was learning about the laws of humanity while I kept on hearing about the abominable ways slaves were treated in Sparta. We pondered the concept of eternity and tried to solve the secrets of the universe, as somber Spartan troops were congregating at our border, bent on destroying our lives and our culture. So how would you have felt in my place? In the place of one whose life, thanks to the laws of Lycurgus, was redeemed at the cost of his mother's life. I felt loathing bubble up within me just hearing the name Sparta.

LEUKOS: I plug up my ears and cover my face, crimson with shame that in the tent of the ephors a Messenean slave is allowed to speak this way.

EUPATOR: Think about the end of it, Spartans. Think about the fact that our long and unsuccessful battles ended triumphantly thanks to Tyrtaeus alone.

TYRTAEUS: Yes, that much I do deserve: a little of your attention. Then you can go on venting you anger, if that's how you
feel. As you know, the war finally broke out between Messene
and Sparta. Your pretext for it was that Messenean shepherds
plucked the fruit off the trees along the border. In truth, the war
was about other things. Sparta was scared that the nearby alien
culture would sooner or later exert influence over the cult of the
muscle. And Messene in turn feared that Sparta would one day
annihilate all that meant as much to them as the laws of Lycurgus
did to Sparta. One or the other had to perish. And why shouldn't
that one be Sparta? Lame as I was, I joined up against Sparta.
Then I fell in captivity and was brought here.

EUPATOR: Awful are the things you're saying, Tyrtaeus. A Spartan can never sink so low as to voice them. And yet we mustn't
forget what you've accomplished for us. Had we been faithful to
our laws, you would no longer be alive. And if you weren't alive,
we wouldn't be alive either. To tell the truth, I don't know which
would have been preferable: to observe the law and thus pass
judgment upon ourselves, or to permit what the law forbids and
thus pass judgment upon the law.

TYRTAEUS: It was as a slave that I returned to Sparta. They
kicked me and spat on me, as is the custom here. I was taken to
the tent of ephor Eupator and began tutoring Demetrios. I can
hardly describe what that task was like. It was like teaching the
tiger not to devour the sheep that was driven to the stream by
thirst. But the boy whose first instructions were in cruelty by
Leukos, started to lean towards other things. And so the lame
one was compelled to realize that it is inhuman laws that turn
people into inhuman beings. The lame one was now in the country of his forefathers. A country that he hated and yet so yearned
to see, because just like the ancestors of Largos, his own ancestors rested in its soil. At that stage he was no longer a Messenean,
nor was he yet a Spartan—because do not forget that according
to the laws of Sparta he would not have been alive. And so, he
was more and more at a loss as to what he should do. He could
not tell his secret to anyone, and there was no one he could ask

for advice. In his soul, he was not yet a Spartan, but the cliffs, the bleak grass, the scarceness of trees and the rarefied air, everything that surrounded him reminded him of how difficult it was to be a Spartan. And how much easier it was to be the son of a more prosperous country. Over here, it was about bare existence. The cows gave little milk. Each portion of millet was so small that eating almost amounted to religious worship. So even as he felt that the meager soup he ate was dark with blood, Bit by bit, his soul was filled with the taste of Sparta. And when he realized that Sparta would lose that last battle, the lame one decided that, rather than betraying his fatherland, he would betray himself. He wrote poems, to inspire the soldiers whom the Spartan discipline had forsaken. He wrote poems and he went into battle, for the sake of a new Sparta.

EUPATOR: He woke the soul of Sparta, just when it seemed that its fist would leave it in the lurch.

PATON: Well, Leukos, what do you say to that?

PHYLO: Speak up, Leukos. You stand before voting citizens. You are also allowed to have your say.

EUPATOR: Let everyone say: Evoe, Tyrtaeus!

TYRTAEUS: It would be wonderful this way, just like in one of those fairytales for children. Evoe, Tyrtaeus, while I stand still. Then when I take a step, it's lame Tyrtaeus. But this is not about my affairs, Spartans—it is about yours. It is about Photina's baby. About a newborn who has a disability.

EUPATOR: The people will grant absolution from the weight of the law.

CROWD: Evoe, Tyrtaeus! (*They surround him; Leukos sneaks over to Phylo*)

LEUKOS: And what am I to do now?

PHYLO: Have them bring in the corpse, fool.

TYRTAEUS: (*Motions for silence with his hands*) Right now, thanks to our victory and to this touching story, you, the people, are feeling benevolent. But the bad days may return to Sparta. Not enough grain and other adversities. And when I'm no longer alive, who will raise his voice on behalf of a tiny child with a disability? Who will speak out for humanity? That's what you Spartans must realize. You have to choose the path upon which you must now travel. And your grasp of it will point the way through many centuries. Because on the highway of humanity there's room for the lame, the paralyzed, the blind and the sick; if they are not crushed under the feet of those whose muscles are unimpaired. Believe it, Sparta, for you to be strong and to preserve your folk culture, you'll need many, many people with a disability—such as the blind poet or the musician who has a hunched back: people whose fate compels them to look inwards. They are not the discus throwers whose discus is flung outwards with the aid of centrifugal force. In them, all human pain travels centripetally towards the depth of the soul. So let them show us, because only humaneness and peace can accomplish miracles on earth. Understandings between peoples, be they Spartans or Messeneans. That rich and poor should not be treated differently. That no one should need fear lawless harassment, or being hauled away as a slave. And that the laws of humans never become rights in the hands of only a few, who use them to rob others of those rights.

LEUKOS: You speak of rights. And the dead—have they no rights at all? Those who died for our ancient laws, are they not entitled to any respect? If they were alive, the lame one would not be able to talk like this! Have the dead got no friends among you at all?! Those who sacrificed their lives are they worth nothing at all? (*He calls out through the opening of the tent*) Bring in the dead! Make way for the dead! (*The crowd, which has been congregating at the opening of the tent, involuntarily separates. Two torchbearers head the procession with flaming torches. The pallbearers bring in the corpse of Nosos. They place him in the middle of the stage in such a way that his head is closest to the opening of the tent, where Phygon is leaning on a naked sword*) Had you any tears left Spartans, they would now fill your eyes at the sight of the corpse of Nosos. But you have no more tears, because you had to weep for so many who died for the fatherland. Dying for the fatherland is a Spartan virtue. It's a virtue that others may mock, because only those are capable of it who do not care how long they live; for whom the only thing that matters is that the fatherland lives. We have no need of learning. We relinquish the kind of reasoning which would lead to Sparta not being Sparta one day. We are cruel towards everything that is gracious and merciful in life and we do not ask for mercy from our enemies. We can lose everything—our lives, our homes, our spouses. There's just one thing we can never lose: our fatherland. The fatherland before anything and above everything. It is easy for those who cannot feel this way to speak of other things. But can we really trust anyone who promises things for which there is no example? Can the most exemplary love of the fatherland be given away for that? We have nothing other than our fatherland, yet no greater treasure exists on earth. So why should we give up this treasure?

TYRTAEUS: The concept of humankind is worth any fatherland.

LEUKOS: Fool. Fantast. Should I love the stranger more than my own kind? Build a roof in mid-air without a structure? We will not change the lifestyle that kept us together so far. Let our ancestors rest in their graves and we will be vigilant in ensuring that the soil of the fatherland is enough for our crops and our graves as well.

PHYLO: Let us swear to it.

CROWD: (*Part of the crowd*) We'll swear to it. Down with Tyrtaeus. (*Others*) Tyrtaeus is right. Enough of suffering.

LEUKOS: Let's vote on it.

TYRTAEUS: No. Let's not vote on it. Because it seems to me that the person who speaks last always carries more weight.

PHYLO: You cannot object to voting, Tyrtaeus. It is democratic that the many should decide upon the truth.

OINOS: And what happens to the truth if it's a tie? Whose truth is it then? And if it's not a tie, what happens to the truth of those who are in the minority? Will they never have their truth?

LEUKOS: What's your answer to that, Tyrtaeus?

TYRTAEUS: That's why I'm saying that we shouldn't vote. How can any one make a decision about the truth, if he is not clear about its essence?

VOICES: Let's vote. Be done with it already. We don't even understand what you're talking about.

TYRTAEUS: (*Sarcastically*) In that case, we really should vote.

LEUKOS: (*Promptly*) Everyone who's present is to vote. Mothers who suckle their babes are to vote on their behalf. Whoever can speak, vote for themselves. (*The crowd gets noisy*)

TYRTAEUS: Good gods, what utter chaos ...

LEUKOS: This isn't chaos. It's the divine people voting. It is true plebiscite.

TYRTAEUS: More like a judgment from the gods, because most of them don't know what they are voting about.

OINOS: I will count the votes—without bias.

LEUKOS: Hands up all those who vote with Sparta against Tyrtaeus. (*Many hands go up*) Count them by tens, Oinos, though you could count them by the hundreds. There are so many of them.

OINOS: (*Counting*) There are six hundred with Leukos.

TINOS: Now count those who didn't put their hands up.

OINOS: (*Counting*) There are six hundred against Leukos.

TYRTAEUS: (*With new hope*) Seeds that are freshly sown can't all be destroyed by the frost.

LEUKOS: (*Suddenly realizing*) But, Oinos, you haven't voted yet.

TYRTAEUS: (*Hopefully*) Oinos ...!

OINOS: (*Standing between the two of them*) My heart pulls me towards you, Tyrtaeus. If I followed my heart I'd vote for you, but I always follow my head. One more vote for Leukos.

LEUKOS: I've won.

TYRTAEUS: You've won. And with those words you just revealed your true ambition. Sparta means no more to you than personal power, which you accomplished by the bewitching language of patriotism.

LEUKOS: We have won. All of you shout twice that we have won. Once against Messene and once in the name of the ancients.

A VOICE: And what'll happen now?

LEUKOS: We'll take Photina's child to the cliffs of Taygetos. (*Three soldiers surround Photina in the crowd. One of them grabs her baby and the other two hold her back. She screams out in anguish*)

A VOICE: And what will happen to Tyrtaeus?

LEUKOS: We'll make him run. He'll be a laughing stock instead of a martyr. Follow me Spartans. (*The crowd departs with Leukos and Phylo in the lead. The pallbearers lift up the stretcher with the corpse of Nosos and exit with it. Photina, almost in a state of delirium, staggers towards the exit. For a second she stops dead in front of Tyrtaeus. But the crowd is pushing her with it. Finally only Oinos is left on the stage with Tyrtaeus*)

TYRTAEUS: (*Looking in the direction of Photina*) May the gods be with you, Photina. Dream that ... (*He waves his hand downwards in a gesture of defeat*)

OINOS: And you, Tyrtaeus, where will you go now?

TYRTAEUS: Where do clouds go? Why don't the rivers surge backwards? And where do the clouds disappear to?

OINOS: Into nothing. But still, where are you going?

TYRTAEUS: I haven't a where. I betrayed Messene; Sparta betrayed me and sooner or later the traitor's path leads to the cliffs of Taygetos.

OINOS: How this is hurting you!

TYRTAEUS: No ...what really hurts me is that your heart should've pulled you towards Sparta, whereas with your head, you should have voted for me. As it is, instead of a new order, I only created chaos.

OINOS: You have to come to terms with it. Leukos has won.

TYRTAEUS: By one vote ...

OINOS: And what if you had won by one vote? Isn't it all the same? Anyway, I have a feeling that neither of you is right. And the day will come when only the ones with brains will be right. I believe in the human brain. Everything points to that.

TYRTAEUS: May the gods be with you.

OINOS: You wanted to be a hero because your lameness bothered your feelings. And now that you're finally leaving the stage, you can't even manage a hero's farewell—something that any bad, itinerant actor could accomplish with ease. Don't you have a wise maxim?

TYRTAEUS: (*An infinite calm spreads over him*) I made a mistake,

Oinos. And there's no maxim wise enough to cover a shocking mistake.

OINOS: What mistake? ... And if you did make a mistake ... it's not ruin, Tyrtaeus?

TYRTAEUS: Only a hero can come to ruin. I'm lame. May the gods be with you. (*He starts to leave*)

OINOS: (*Fighting back tears*) A person who leaves like that must have been right. Forgive me, Tyrtaeus. I made a mistake when voting and it was your ruin. (*Crying, he rushes after the crowd*)

TYRTAEUS: (*Very shaken, he stops. Once again, he feels something like a calling*) Sparta, you've won. But if you remain as you are, according to the laws of progress you will have to perish. Because a time will come when the mighty will be weak compared to the might of the weak, and the truth will belong to everyone. (*He exists stage right ... a light breeze causes the empty tent to quiver. Then the curtain slowly comes down*)

THE END

TRANSLATOR'S AFTERWORD

In the late 1930s and early 1940s, inspired by Sándor Pethö's famous editorial, entitled "Athens and Sparta," the Hungarian intelligentsia tended to symbolically equate ancient Sparta with German fascism, and ancient Athens with Western democracy. Given the strong educational focus on Latin and Greek culture in Hungary at the time, moreover, matters classical—from Homer's epics to the tragedy of Athens to the rise of Rome and beyond—were common cultural currency. As renowned critic Géza Hegedüs succinctly puts it: "Alcaeus, Sappho, Anacreon and Tyrtaeus approached the closeness of friends."

Thus, when Lajos Walder decided to hark back to the distant past to mirror and refract the present in his play *Tyrtaeus*, he was well acquainted with the ancient world. He knew that the elegiac seventh-century poet Tyrtaeus spoke and wrote in the Doric dialect (the language of both Sparta and Messene); that, after Callinus, he was the earliest-known practitioner of the lyric genre of the battle hymn; and that during the Second Messenean war in the mid-seventh century BCE, he was elected, by oracular decree, to head the victorious Spartan troops, whom he inspired with soul-stirring song.

Of course, the ages have handed down many contrasting anecdotes about Tyrtaeus, on which the playwright could freely draw. Some of them claim that Tyrtaeus was a lame schoolmaster from Athens. Others suggest that, like Callinus, he was a native Milesian. Yet in view of Tyrtaeus' use of the Doric dialect in his surviving poetic fragments, all of which treat of war and the virtue of dying for one's country (e. g. fragments 6 and 7), linguists hold that he was either a native Spartan or born somewhere near Sparta in the Peloponnese.

Sparta Around 700 B.C.E.

Instead of urbanizing like most of ancient Greece, the city-state of Sparta was made up of a complex of five village settlements. It was ruled by two kings. Five ephors, or overseers—elected annually to represent the five villages—greatly curtailed the executive powers of the two kings and eventually replaced them entirely in presiding over the assembly of citizens.

Unlike other Greek city-states, Sparta substituted military conquest for overseas migration to solve the problem of its growing need for land. Central Messene's fertile plains were among the richest in Greece. Following its conquest, the victorious Spartans divided the land into lots for distribution among their countrymen, while turning the defeated Messeneans into helots, or slaves. In the mid-seventh century, the Messeneans rose up against their Spartan oppressors, who crushed their revolt in the so-called Second Messenean War. In order to continue controlling Messene, however—of the total population, Spartans numbered only one in fifteen—Sparta had to reorganize its own society, adopting an even more military-focused lifestyle.

Political privilege was reserved exclusively for Spartans, whose citizenship rights were based on birth and the possession of family lots. While the circle of citizenship was tight, within it Spartans enjoyed a considerable degree of equality. The strict regimentation of Spartan life helped to preserve the city-state's identity and secure its continued dominion over helots and peasant serfs, on whose labor it depended.

The Spartan system was designed to rid itself of the 'weak', to train the Spartan male for war, and to keep him in constant readiness for it. At birth, each baby was subjected to an examination by a board of inspectors. If the child was found to be weak or imperfect, it was abandoned on the cliffs of mount Taygetos. Education was carefully designed to prevent the formation of attachments other than to the state. The rigorous training of male children began early. They were taught to fend for themselves, if need be by stealing, and to endure the hardships of long marches and cruel rites of initiation without complaint. In their teenage years, the boys were required to kill a helot as part of their training. Helots, therefore, lived in constant fear for their lives. The boys also functioned as part of the *crypteia*, the Spartan secret police. Age groups were strictly segregated, and disciplinary measures, enforced by older boys, were overseen by special officials who were youth trainers known as *paidagogoi*. Save for battle hymns and a few lines from Homer (used as moral maxims) Spartan boys received no humanistic education. Girls went through gymnastics training, and it was not considered immodest for females to exercise virtually in the nude. At the age of twenty, males became active soldiers and lived together in barracks. At the age of thirty, marriage was permitted, but family life was kept to a minimum. The Spartan male then joined a military mess of fifteen men. He lived in a tightly knit group of fellow fighters, often bound by erotic affection that far outweighed the value of wife and children.

Such training produced highly courageous and tough soldiers, and Spartan military skill and discipline won the respect of all the other Greek states. Although he criticized Sparta's strictly military aim, Plato was respectful of the controlled workings of its system. Thus, in The Republic, he expressed his admiration for Lycurgus. No one knows definitively whether Lycurgus—Sparta's legendary lawgiver and national father figure—was a real or mythical person; but he certainly enjoyed virtually divine status among Spartans (as did the Führer among his subjects in Nazi Germany some 2500 years later).

In *The Histories*, Herodotus writes that in the past, Spartans, who "would have no dealings with any kind of strangers," had been both externally and internally the worst governed people. But Lycurgus was to change all that. "Lycurgus, a distinguished Spartan, visited the Delphic oracle, and no sooner had he entered the shrine than he was greeted with these words:

'Hither to my rich temple have you come, Lycurgus,
Dear to Zeus and to all gods that dwell on Olympus.

Tyrtaeus: A Tragedy

> I know not whether to declare you human or divine—
> Yet I incline to believe, Lycurgus, that you are a god.'

Herodotus also mentions that, according to one story, the priestess of the temple revealed to Lycurgus the system of government that he subsequently introduced in Sparta. Yet the Lacedaemonians, as the Spartans were also known, claimed that Lycurgus—who, as the guardian of his nephew, King Leobotas, became Regent of Sparta—had brought his system of government from Crete.

Although tough and disciplined in war, the Spartans were grossly limited in other ways. They did not put a premium on developing the imagination or the ability to reason. Trained in brevity of speech, they were particularly poor at self-expression, as our own word 'laconic'—deriving from 'Laconia', the Peloponnesian region that also includes Sparta—still attests. Nor could the Spartans cope with the political consequences of the occupation and wars they wrought. Interestingly, Spartan fighters readied themselves for battle with flute playing, and wrote their names on a piece of white cloth that they wrapped around their left arm, which allowed the war dead to be identified.

Important Analogies with Fascism and Nazi Ideology in the Play

Benito Mussolini rose to power in Italy in 1922 and became the first fascist dictator. His irredentist nationalism quickly won favor in Hungary, a country still badly hurting from the loss of many of its territories following the defeat of Germany and the Austro-Hungarian Empire in World War I and the Treaty of Trianon in 1920.

The character of Leukos, the play's Spartan youth trainer, embodies the Italian dictator's (and, ironically, erstwhile elementary school teacher's) unscrupulous ways and love for dramatic posturing.

Mussolini named his party after the Latin 'fasces' (pl. of 'fascis'), a classical Roman symbol of authority consisting of a bundle wooden rods, sometimes containing a projecting axe blade. Its symbolic message was simple: While a single rod can easily be broken, many rods tied together present an unbreakable force. Fascism thrived on the ignorance of the masses, whose emotional incitement was made easier by keeping them in the dark. Similarly, the character of Lukianos is so ignorant that he cannot even count to six. He refers to himself as "the whip," and metes out punishment at Leukos' command.

A totalitarian form of government, fascism did not tolerate any kind of opposition or dissent, crushing it with the help of its secret police. All aspects of social-political life—the economy, education, athletics, recreation etc.—were brought under the strict control of the state, which cultivated and relied on its subjects' ignorance. To maintain popular consent, fascist leadership had to bar the people from access to any information that might result in questioning the powers that be. Thus, Leukos makes an example of the innocent youth Teknon because he is more astute and discriminating than the other boys. In the process, the youth trainer not only strikes one of Mussolini's best-known poses in turning his back to a terrified twelve-year old with legs apart and arms folded across his chest, feigning bravery, but he also imitates Mussolini's overall histrionics.

The highly emotional content of his opportunistic and depraved speeches, furthermore—both to the children he trains at the beginning of the play, and to the crowd he manipulates at the end of it—also conjure Hitler's speeches, with their effective subversion of truth through bombastic rhetoric. As Tyrtaeus remarks to ephor Eupator: "People will often give power to those who appeal to their emotions and not to reason." Sadly, even today, in the twenty-first century, the universal truth of this statement will readily be acknowledged. But around 1940, when the play was written, it had a particularly chilling effect amid the German and Hungarian Nazi onslaught. The character of Leukos also recalls the leaders of the Hitler Youth in his encouragement of male bonding and eroticism as a means of molding Sparta's future fighters (even if this entails the rape of a young boy). Indeed, one of Nazi Germany's many paradoxes consisted in the fact that, whilst homosexuals were officially persecuted, many of the leaders of the Hitler Youth were homosexuals themselves. Pertinently, the character of Photina, pleading for her baby before the ephors, has the following to say about Lycurgus:

> In vain he preaches about the glories of pregnancy and carries on about solstice celebrations for boys, when what he would really have liked is fighters giving birth to armed fighters. That's why he secretly prescribed that they should love each other. If they were able to conceive, perhaps then he could successfully control nature and avoid reproduction's slow, protracted course.

The *Sonnenwende Feier*, or summer solstice celebration, which was mandatory for all Hitler Youth, had highly erotic overtones. Similar bonding rituals for young males to prepare them for war were also common in ancient Sparta, which had served as the *de facto* model for the very institution of the Hitler Youth. Fascism aimed to keep the population in a constant war-like state of mind. Every citizen had to be made to feel perpetually mobilized against enemies of the regime both from within and without.

When explaining the plausibility of the Spartan custom of stealing, together with its severe punishment, Leukos tells Demetrios:

> Elsewhere, thieves are the most cowardly, but with us only the bravest steal because one must have enormous courage to stake one's life on a few apples or some bad poultry. We Spartans revolve in constant danger; therefore we have to live dangerously, so we can train ourselves for the dangers that lurk all around us. You can hardly fulfill the imperative to live dangerously more thoroughly than by risking your life to obtain everything that goes into your daily soup. This state makes you so alert that in a split-second you are in readiness to overthrow anyone who threatens your life.

Historically, fascist dictators such as Hitler and Mussolini, came to power during periods of economic crisis. Following its defeat in World War I, Germany went through one economic crisis after another and, as in *Tyrtaeus'* fictional Sparta, "the millet was sparse." The dictator must convince his people that the country is under threat. At the start of World War II, in order to invade Poland, Hitler fabricated the excuse of Polish border aggression. Sparta's excuse for the conquest of Messene in *Tyrtaeus* consists in the allegation that Messenean shepherds plucked fruit from Spartan trees along the border.

Sparta's presumed supremacy, as propounded by Lycurgus, mirrors Nazi Germany's belief in the supremacy of the Aryan race. Nazi propaganda relentlessly caricatured and degraded the Jews and other peoples and cultures, so as to make them easier to hate. The character of Phygon—a hysterical Spartan youth who flagellates himself in the name of discipline and "loves Sparta to the point of madness"—could be one of those fervent Hitler youths. When, in the first scene, Oinos sights five utterly exhausted and wounded prisoners of war, who are being herded by two Spartan soldiers, Phygon, without having seen them, promises to personally stave in their heads and "gouge their eyes out" because "their cheeks are like the jowls of horses and they have the hearts of wolves" and "devour babies." Shortly thereafter, he shouts: "Oh beloved Sparta! Awful Huns have ambushed our beautiful fatherland." And despite repeated confirmation that only five prisoners have been taken, Phygon continues to insist that "they number a thousand," and with Leukos' encouragement goes off to spread the mendacious news that "thousands and thousands of new prisoners have arrived in Sparta."

Dovetailing with Phygon's rabid nationalism, his fanatic, disciplinarian grandfather, commander Nosos, asserts that his "god is Sparta," which echoes the Hitlerite principle of 'country before God'. Later in the play, when Nosos' corpse is brought in, Leukos manipulates the crowd with a soul-stirring speech about the fatherland. Here is an excerpt from that address:

Dying for the fatherland is a Spartan virtue. It's a virtue that others may mock, because only those are capable of it who do not care how long they live; for whom the only thing that matters is that the fatherland lives ... We can lose everything—our lives, our home, our spouses. There's just one thing we can never lose: our fatherland. The fatherland before anything and above everything. It is easy for those who cannot feel this way to speak of other things. But can we really trust anyone who promises things for which there is no example? Can the most exemplary love of the fatherland be given away for that? We have nothing other than our fatherland, yet no greater treasure exists on earth. So why should we give up this treasure?

In interwar Hungary, the idea of humankind, or rather 'humanism', continually clashed with a distorted version of patriotism. One of the basic tenets of national-socialist, arrow-cross ideology—the Arrow Cross Party was the Hungarian national-socialist party—held that whoever considered humankind more important than his country was a traitor. The so-called 'humanists' were branded as everything from 'left-wing' to 'bourgeois' to 'liberal' to 'radical'. They were considered 'unpatriotic' and 'alien'—labels that easily morphed into 'Jew'. Appositely, in response to Leukos' invective, Tyrtaeus observes: "The concept of humankind is worth any fatherland."

Early on in the play, Pharon, the epitome of the ideal Spartan soldier, returns home a starving, disillusioned veteran of many lost battles. When Tyrtaeus questions him, he is hard-pressed to explain what it means to him to be a Spartan, and why he is fighting for it, because concepts elude his combat-trained mind. He then flares up and says, alluding to the deliberately spectacular military parades that have since become the hallmark of the Third Reich:

If you had seen how beautiful it was when a thousand divisions goose-stepped at the parade, in front of our leader. A thousand times fifteen men. The crests of their helmets were shining. Their bellies were full; shoulder was taut against shoulder. And the earth thundered. Yes, now I do know what being a Spartan means to me.

But when Tyrtaeus reminds Pharon that not even a hundred divisions remain of the thousand, that his belly is empty and that the only thing left is the gleam of his helmet, we witness the playwright's prescience as to Nazi Germany's eventual defeat.

Hitlerism espoused that women should stay home and bear children in order to propagate the perfect Aryan race. There was, of course, an added benefit for the regime: The combination of rearmament and the removal of women from the work force helped to eliminate unemployment. The notion that it was women's patriotic duty to produce children for the state was so ingrained during the Third Reich that many young women became pregnant just to fulfill this duty. Nazi propaganda continually encouraged them to give babies to the Führer. Many a married woman, too, had but few scruples obeying this order, even if it meant violating the sanctity of marriage. Ninety percent of illegitimate babies born in the Third Reich were raised in so-called *Lebensborn* ('*river-of-life*') homes. Illegitimacy was no longer a disgrace. A couple's racial purity was the prime concern. Thus, the character of Photina reminds Tyrtaeus of Lycurgus' decree to the effect that "women cook the soup and give birth to children," and compares her womanly duty to that of a cow. And in her earlier-quoted expostulation on Lycurgus' account, she highlights the "glories of pregnancy," irrespective of the partner, and points out that the "law consents to a pause only when conception has occurred." Concomitantly, she avers that she exercised "just so I'd become faultless, and have the seed faultless within me; the seed that would one day ripen into a son." In Nazi Germany, too, women were encouraged to exercise for the sole purpose of breeding the perfect race.

The fictional Tyrtaeus is imbued with the humanistic values of his author: a modern poet and playwright of the 1930s and early 1940s, and a trained attorney, who, though admitted to the bar in 1937, was never allowed to practice following the passing of the Jewish laws in Hungary. "... according to the demands of racial purity / I can't officially prove // that I am actually descended from Adam," Walder poignantly observes in the poem "Coming to Terms with the Impossible" (published in *Become a Message: Poems*, New York, 2015). And so, for a brief moment in Act I, Scene 3—it's the middle of the night—the play's protagonist becomes one with his creator in the hope of being able to ameliorate the human condition through education, one of Lajos Walder's central concerns.

The fictional Tyrtaeus' legally sound philosophical arguments were extraordinary for his times, especially considering the playwright's own circumstances as he crafted them: For as the fictional Tyrtaeus defines justice as "a condition in which everyone can do what anyone else can do, and no one has to endure what he himself mustn't commit"; as he states that "in the hands of a single individual, only the sum total of the rights due to him guarantees natural law, which is the right of every human being," his author's rights were being rescinded one by one. Tyrtaeus' legal and ethical points are valid to this day, even on the other side of the world; and his comments on the individual's ability to increase his portion of natural law and the fundamental goods of human flourishing fill us with hope more than seventy years on.

Eupator bitterly remarks to Tyrtaeus that "many of those who fight under the Messenenan flag rally under it only to fight against Sparta," to which Tyrtaeus replies, alluding to the partisans of various nationalities who rallied against the Nazis: "This is a battle of democracy, my lord." And as things on the battlefield are going disastrously for Sparta, Nosos tells Eupator that he must lower the conscription age to twelve—a chilling reference to the Nazi's lowering the age of conscription to fifteen toward the end of the war. The last scene of Act 2 ends with the start of the battle. An original segment of one of Tyrtaeus' surviving battle hymns is recited to the accompaniment of the Marseillaise—the quintessential freedom anthem among the educated members of the Hungarian bourgeoisie.

One of my father's strongest-held personal beliefs consisted in the ongoing need for progress. I know that he saw it as a way to help to ensure our humanity. In Act 1, Scene 3, when he most resembles his creator, Tyrtaeus attempts to convince Eupator to make peace and guide Sparta towards progress. His valid criticism of democracy and its shortcomings, especially that it can be harnessed for racist-nationalist dictatorial ends—Hitler had been democratically elected, after all—is signally relevant in our own twenty-first century. As Tyrtaeus points out to Eupator, general voting rights "can be a very dangerous tool in the hands of a clever demagogue and a lot of ignorant and unthinking voters." Over seventy years ago, under a virulently national-socialist Hungarian government, Lajos Walder presaged the necessity of what today is readily acknowledged by Western democracies: The granting of citizenship should require at least a basic knowledge of the constitution of the given country.

Photina is Tyrtaeus' soul mate and personal oracle. Her womanly soul, "much more refined than the soul of a man," sees early on that Tyrtaeus will "err with the decisive step," that the unbending ways of Sparta will not condone his vision of a new and more humane society. And when Tyrtaeus tries to save Photina's baby, stressing that a person with a disability may well bring honor to his country, ephor Phylo eagerly rallies behind him in obliquely invoking a famous orator who, despite his speech impediment, had become the finest orator of his country. (Demosthenes is said to have put a pebble in his mouth to overcome his stuttering.)

Operating on numerous levels, *Tyrtaeus* also delivers on its implicit original promise of being a Greek tragedy. The play's fictionalized poet forgets what his author never forgot: that the first task of a poet is clarity of vision—that a gift of extraordinary insight must never be compromised. The protagonist's own tragedy consists in the fact that he falls prey to his personal longings. And as in all Greek tragedy, his suffering turns out to be of the bitterest kind when he learns that the victory he has wrought has brought about the opposite of what he had fought for.

For all that, the author's vision remains crystal-clear. How could the hero possibly triumph when, in the early 1940s, the playwright saw no reprieve for humanity for some time to come.

A final word on Lajos Walder's wonderful sense of humor, which palpably manifest itself in the play in a memorable quip on the theater he loved so much. As the people of Sparta are panicking on the edge of ruin, their newly elected commander Tyrtaeus muses: "I must arouse the people's emotions in any way I can. That's why I've never gone to the theater. So I wouldn't witness the inducement of true emotions through untrue words."

Available and forthcoming from UWSP

- *November Rose: A Speech on Death* by Kathrin Stengel
  (2008 Independent Publisher Book Award)
- *November-Rose: Eine Rede über den Tod* by Kathrin Stengel
- *Philosophical Fragments of a Contemporary Life* by Julien David
- *17 Vorurteile, die wir Deutschen gegen Amerika und die Amerikaner
  haben und die so nicht ganz stimmen können* by Misha Waiman
- *The DNA of Prejudice: On the One and the Many*
  by Michael Eskin (2010 Next Generation Indie Book Award
  for Social Change)
- *Descartes' Devil: Three Meditations* by Durs Grünbein
- *Fatal Numbers: Why Count on Chance*
  by Hans Magnus Enzensberger
- *The Vocation of Poetry* by Durs Grünbein
  (2011 Independent Publisher Book Award)
- *Mortal Diamond: Poems* by Durs Grünbein
- *Yoga for the Mind: A New Ethic for Thinking and Being
  & Meridians of Thought* by Michael Eskin & Kathrin Stengel
  (2014 Living Now Book Award)
- *Health Is In Your Hands: Jin Shin Jyutsu – Practicing the Art of Self-
  Healing (With 51 Flash Cards for the Hands-on Practice of Jin Shin
  Jyutsu)* by Waltraud Riegger-Krause (2015 Living Now Book
  Award for Healing Arts)
- *The Wisdom of Parenthood: An Essay* by Michael Eskin
- *A Moment More Sublime: A Novel* by Stephen Grant
  (2015 Independent Publisher Book Award for Contemporary
  Fiction)
- *High on Low: Harnessing the Power of Unhappiness*
  by Wilhelm Schmid (2015 Living Now Book Award for
  Personal Growth & 2015 Independent Publisher Book Award
  for Self-Help)

- *Become a Message: Poems* by Lajos Walder
  (2016 Benjamin Franklin Book Award for Poetry)
- *What We Gain As We Grow Older: On Gelassenheit*
  by Wilhelm Schmid
- *On Dialogic Speech* by L. P. Yakubinsky
- *Passing Time: An Essay on Waiting* by Andrea Köhler
- *In Praise of Weakness* by Alexandre Jollien
- *Vase of Pompeii: A Play* by Lajos Walder
- *Below Zero: A Play* by Lajos Walder
- *Tyrtaeus: A Tragedy* by Lajos Walder
- *The Complete Plays* by Lajos Walder
- *Homo Conscius: A Novel* by Timothy Balding
- *Castile: A Novel* by Stephen Grant
- *Potentially Harmless: A Philosopher's Manhattan*
  by Kathrin Stengel